Sunset

ideas for great

FLOORS

By the Editors of
Sunset Books

Sunset Books ■ Menlo Park, California

Sunset Books

vice president, general manager:
Richard A. Smeby

vice president, editorial director:
Bob Doyle

production director:
Lory Day

art director:
Vasken Guiragossian

Staff for this book:

developmental editor:
Linda J. Selden

editor:
Linda Hetzer

text:
Marie Tupot Stock

art direction:
Areta Buk/Thumb Print

photo research:
Toby Greenberg

shopper's guide photography:
Tom Haynes

illustrations:
Eileen Whalen

production assistant:
Sara Newberry

cover design:
Vasken Guiragossian

Ideas for Great Floors

was produced in conjunction with Roundtable Press, Inc.
Directors: Marsha Melnick, Susan E. Meyer, Julie Merberg

First printing June 2002
Copyright ©2002, Sunset Books, Inc.,
Menlo Park, CA 94025. First edition. All rights
reserved, including the right of reproduction in whole
or in part in any form.

ISBN 0-376-01178-5
Library of Congress Control Number 2001098868
First edition.
Printed in the United States.

For additional copies of Ideas for Great Floors or any
other Sunset Book, call 1-800-526-5111.
Or see our website at: www.sunsetbooks.com

A firm foundation

A good book is a great place to start when embarking on a flooring project. With the broad range of incredible flooring available today, it's practically a must. After all, no matter the size of the project, no one wants a plain old floor anymore.

We hope this book from our "Ideas for Great" series leads you to the floor covering of your dreams. Once you've seen all the choices presented in the pages that follow, you'll see there's no reason to settle for less.

Many individuals and firms were expert resources for us in planning this book. We're particularly indebted to Hal Tupot of Custom Modern Tile & Construction, Bob Daniels of The Tile Council of America, Melissa Watkins, Cathy Gutkowski, Mark Frolich and Marge Ventura of the Expo Design Center, Union, NJ, Carol Swedlow of Aronson's, Jan MacLatchie of Artistic Tile, and Brian J. Sakosits and Robert W. Sanzari of Hoboken Floors.

We would also like to thank Ray Wolf of Home Depot and Halina Switzer of Nemo Tile. Credits for specific product shots are listed on page 126.

contents

on which we stand

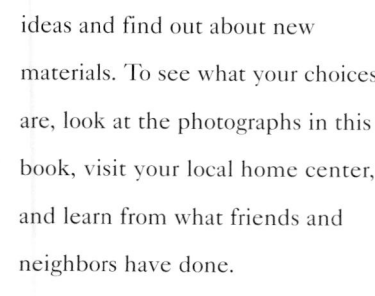

WITH MOST THINGS in life, it's the basics that count. And a floor is basic not only to the structure of any room but also to its design. Your floor has to look beautiful and it has to work.

After the walls, the floor is the next largest surface in a room, and you'll want to give it the same careful attention that you give to any other design element. When choosing flooring, you'll probably think first about your options. You'll want to learn about stone, tile, wood, resilient, carpet, laminate, and concrete. You may even want to think outside the box, as they say, and consider such specialty flooring materials as leather or metal.

Take a look at what's out there. There is a new attitude toward flooring materials. No longer is tile necessary for the kitchen and wood a must for the living room. Today a living room floor can be tiled, a bathroom looks great in stone, and a kitchen is warmed by a wood floor. Stay open to new ideas and find out about new materials. To see what your choices are, look at the photographs in this book, visit your local home center, and learn from what friends and neighbors have done.

As you look at these choices, you'll find that each type of material is rich in color, texture, and pattern. Will a light color floor that exudes spaciousness capture your attention? Or will you choose a dark floor that anchors a room's furnishings and allows them to take center stage? Do you want the floor to have a pattern that takes command in the room, or will you

choose a floor that fits an existing design scheme? Are there special features you want to highlight—in a foyer, a dining room, or around a fireplace?

Keeping all these design options in mind, you'll want to focus on the room's function. Think about how your family uses the room. What activities happen there? Who spends time in the room—and how much foot traffic will there be? Where will the furniture be placed? And how much time are you willing to spend maintaining the floor?

The flooring choices you make now will affect the way your house works for you and your family. With a little planning, you'll find that there's a flooring choice that's right for you—one that is beautiful and complements the design of your home while it meets all your practical needs, and that everyone loves to walk on!

A PLANNING PRIMER

FLOORS. You walk on them daily, hardly ever giving a second thought to what's underfoot until the day you realize it's time to make a change. Suddenly there are countless decisions to be made. First, you need to select the right type of flooring for the specific area in your home. What will look best in the space? What will work best over time? What will be practical, easy to keep clean? USE THIS CHAPTER to guide you through all the steps you'll need to consider before making the right choice of floor covering. The more you know about flooring, the more satisfied you'll be with your choice. For a quick overview of what's available, go to the chart "Comparing Flooring" on pages 12–13. By the end of this chapter, you'll be able to comfortably decide which direction to take and whether to install the flooring yourself or hire a professional. Now's the time to start exploring new ideas for flooring.

exploring your options

TODAY *it's virtually impossible to say one type of flooring is appropriate to a specific room. Whether it's tile, stone, wood, resilient, carpeting, or laminate, new technologies have made most flooring adaptable to all kinds of situations. Still, there are plenty of practicalities to consider when you are planning to install a new floor. Take the time to decide on a floor that both inspires you now and fits all your practical needs.*

What's available?

Centuries ago fabulous floors belonged only to royalty and could be created only by the most talented craftsmen. Today we have many incredible flooring materials available. Each material possesses its own inherent qualities and when skillfully installed can evoke any feeling or achieve any look. Better yet, some of the least expensive materials can have the most powerful impact for your floor.

TILE is one of the fastest-growing flooring materials in the United States. Ceramic flooring pavers, terra-cotta, and charming mosaics in all shapes and sizes are quite familiar, but tiles have also become diverse. New products on the market today include metal tiles, photographic tiles, glass tiles, porcelain pavers, and custom tiles. Flooring tile differs from wall tile—one should not be used in place of the other. Flooring tile has a lower water absorption rate and consequently a denser body. The denser body makes the tile strong enough to walk on. Because of its low water absorption and easy maintenance, homeowners traditionally select tile for kitchens and bathrooms, but it is also finding a niche in living rooms.

STONE flooring comes from quarries mostly in Italy, Spain, Turkey, and the United States. Each type of natural stone, from marble to granite to slate, features a unique color, pattern, and hardness. Natural stone is available both as smoothly cut tiles and irregular slabs. Either can be finished to be smooth as glass or tumbled for a timeworn appearance.

A colorful terrazzo tiled floor in a children's playroom serves as a strong and forgiving backdrop for playtime fun. Not only does the floor allow for easy maintenance, but its contemporary styling won't be outgrown during the teen years.

Choosing a variety of flooring materials for one room is a creative option. In this modern home, neutral limestone tiles underscore the living area while hardwood flooring covers the common areas nearby, including an open staircase.

The color choices of stone are endless. You'll find marble in black, cream, red, white, green, gold, gray, and even pink. Some types of marble are heavily veined, such as Nero Marquina, with its ebony color and white veining, while others, such as Golden Spider, are lightly veined. Still others, such as Yellow Desert, look somewhat dappled, as if they were sponge finished. There are also creamy soft and classic types, like Crema Marfil.

If you prefer this softer appearance, you also may like limestone, which is usually light-colored, with a speckled surface. Granite, while having the same breadth of colors as marble, looks more mottled. If you like more irregular stones, you should consider flagstone, which can be reminiscent of medieval castle floors.

Stone can be costly, so you'll want to use it where it makes the most impact in your home. A stone floor in a foyer or entryway, for instance, makes a great first impression on guests.

WOOD is warm and inviting and feels good underfoot. Wood flooring is available in a variety of species, from pine and bamboo to maple and oak. It comes prefinished, unfinished, solid, engineered, reclaimed, in parquet and in planks, and in varying grades and cuts. Wood planks range from a narrow 3 inches to a wide 20 inches and can be finished with a penetrating seal or a surface seal. In addition, there are a number of

ABOVE: Sometimes, a little texture can make all the difference. A practical choice, richly textured vinyl looks right at home running across the entire floor of a southwestern kitchen and dining room. RIGHT: In a subtle blend of two textures, tumbled limestone tiles and decorative metal inserts, are used to create a border design.

prefabricated decorative borders and medallions that can be inlaid into a wood floor as a unit.

Throughout history, wood flooring has been used in residential living areas. If you love the look of wood flooring but think something more insulating would perform better, consider a wood floor complemented by an area rug. You might also consider wood for less-used bathrooms, such as a powder room or a guest bath.

RESILIENT flooring consists of vinyl and linoleum, as well as rubber and cork. Most popular today is vinyl. The focus for resilient vinyl flooring has been on increasing its durability and performance while also developing more natural-looking materials, and the result is a variety of great-looking and long-lasting products. Linoleum came on the scene about 50 years ago. Made from a mixture of ground wood, cork, linseed oil, and resin, it fell out of favor but is now enjoying a resurgence. The resilient category also encompasses rubber and cork flooring. Available in sheets or tiles (cork is also made as a floating floor system), resilient flooring is easy to install and can be cut in a variety of imaginative shapes.

Resilient flooring performs well in hard-working areas such as kitchens, mudrooms, and laundry rooms. And with its imaginative new designs and patterns, resilient flooring can be terrific in a playroom.

LAMINATE flooring debuted in the early 1980s in Sweden. A high-pressure melamine that is installed as a floating floor, a laminate consists of a base of several layers of paper impregnated with resins. A top layer of decorative paper determines the design, which means if something can be photographed, it can be laminated. The first laminates emulated hardwood floors, but now you can find laminates that look like marble, granite, and ceramic tile. Early laminates had a tendency to chip or delaminate, but durability has been significantly improved and warrantees have been extended accordingly. Glueless laminates that click into place are now available.

Use a laminate wherever you want versatility in performance and a clean, unfettered look.

New stain-resistant options allow broadloom carpeting to be used in places where it was previously discouraged, such as dining rooms. Even red wine doesn't pose a threat to light-colored carpets anymore, provided that the carpet has been treated.

It runs beautifully across wide-open great rooms flowing from kitchen to dining to living areas.

CARPETING today is much more than the traditional loop pile we know so well. New technologies have allowed for more texture and surface interest, as well as multiple colors and overall patterns. Loop styles include level loop, multilevel, cut pile, and cut-and-loop patterns. Designs can be sculpted so they appear to pop out. Synthetic fibers are more pleasant to the touch. Custom carpet installers expand design options further, and for carpet padding, manufacturers are working with postconsumer waste to introduce environmentally friendly products. With its cushioning comfort and ability to absorb sound, carpeting is often the first choice for bedrooms.

SPECIALTY flooring uses materials commonly found in industrial and commercial structures, such as concrete, leather, and steel, but are now coming into vogue for high-end residential flooring. Concrete has received the most field testing to date. Appreciated for its ability to take on shape and color, concrete has been embraced by interior designers and architects. It is especially favored for kitchens and dining areas. Leather tiles have typically been used as a novelty to accent a room. Because leather is a natural material, no two tiles are alike and the floor will develop a patina as it ages. Leather should be used only in areas of the home that have little traffic, such as formal living rooms. Steel flooring is available as sleek oversized tiles or industrial grating. It makes a stylish complement to industrial-style kitchens outfitted with stainless steel appliances. Decorative metal pieces are also available as accents for concrete or tile floors.

COMPARING FLOORING

Each type of flooring material has its intrinsic properties. Since a variety of materials will work in each room of the house, you can use this chart to compare the properties of the flooring materials you're considering.

CERAMIC TILE

ADVANTAGES. Made from hard-fired slabs of clay, ceramic tile is available in hundreds of patterns, colors, shapes, and finishes. Its durability, easy upkeep, and attractiveness are definite advantages. Tiles are usually classified as quarry tiles, commonly unglazed red-clay tiles that are rough and water resistant; terra-cotta, unglazed tiles in earth-tone shades; porcelain pavers, rugged tiles in stonelike shades and textures; and glazed floor tiles, available in glossy, matte, and textured finishes. Floor tiles run the gamut of widths, lengths, and thicknesses. Most popular are 8-inch and 12-inch squares. Costs range from inexpensive to moderate; in general, porcelain is most expensive. Tiles made of purer clays and fired at higher temperatures are generally costlier but better wearing.

DISADVANTAGES. Tile can be cold, noisy, and depending on its "co-efficient of friction," slippery underfoot. Porous tiles become stained and harbor bacteria unless properly sealed. Grout can be tough to keep clean, though mildew-resistant and epoxy types are easier.

EXPECTED LIFESPAN. Lifetime

MOST APPROPRIATE LOCATIONS. Kitchens, baths, foyers, mudrooms

APPROXIMATE COST PER SQUARE FOOT. $2.50 to $8.00

STONE

ADVANTAGES. Natural stone (such as slate, marble, limestone, and granite) has been used as flooring for centuries. Today its use is even more practical, thanks to the development of efficient sealers and better surfacing techniques. Stone can be used in its natural shape, known as flagstone, or cut into rectangular blocks or tiles. Generally, pieces are butted tightly together; irregular flagstones require wider grout joints.

DISADVANTAGES. The cost of masonry flooring can be quite high, though recent diamond-saw technology has lowered it considerably. Moreover, the weight of the materials requires a very strong, well-supported subfloor. Some stone is cold and slippery underfoot, though new honed and etched surfaces are safer, subtler alternatives to polished surfaces. Certain stones, such as marble and limestone, absorb stains and dirt readily. Careful sealing is essential.

EXPECTED LIFESPAN. Lifetime

MOST APPROPRIATE LOCATIONS. Kitchens, bathrooms, foyers

APPROXIMATE COST PER SQUARE FOOT. $3.00 to $10.00

HARDWOOD

ADVANTAGES. A classic hardwood floor is warm, feels good underfoot, and can be refinished. Oak is most common, with maple, birch, pine, bamboo, and other woods also available. The three basic types of flooring are narrow strips in random lengths; planks in various widths and random lengths; and tiles laid in blocks or squares. Wood flooring may be factory prefinished or unfinished, to be sanded and finished in place. "Floating" floor systems have several veneered strips atop each backing board. In addition, premanufactured hardwood medallions can be purchased separately and incorporated into the floor design. Engineered wood flooring is more dimensionally stable and may be more compatible than solid wood in moisture-prone areas.

DISADVANTAGES. Moisture damage and inadequate floor substructure are two potential problems to consider. Maintenance is another issue; some surfaces can be mopped or waxed while others cannot. Bleaching and some staining processes may wear unevenly and are difficult to repair. Costs are moderate to high, depending on wood species, grade, and finish.

EXPECTED LIFESPAN. Lifetime

MOST APPROPRIATE LOCATIONS. Living rooms, dining rooms, bedrooms, foyers

APPROXIMATE COST PER SQUARE FOOT. $2.50 to $8.50

RESILIENT

ADVANTAGES. Generally made from solid vinyl or polyurethane, resilients are flexible, moisture and stain resistant, easy to install, and simple to maintain. Available in a great variety of colors, textures, patterns, and styles, tiles can be mixed to form custom patterns or provide color accents. Sheets run up to 12 feet wide, eliminating the need for seaming; tiles are generally 12 inches square. Vinyl, cork, and rubber are comfortable to walk on. A polyurethane finish may eliminate the need for waxing. Costs are generally modest, but expect to pay a premium for custom or imported products.

DISADVANTAGES. Resilients are relatively soft, making them vulnerable to dents and tears; often, though, such damage can be repaired. Tiles may collect moisture between seams if improperly installed. Some vinyl still comes with a photographically applied pattern, but most is inlaid; the latter is more expensive but wears much better.

EXPECTED LIFESPAN. 20 to 30 years

MOST APPROPRIATE LOCATIONS. Kitchens, baths, work and play areas

APPROXIMATE COST PER SQUARE FOOT. $1.00 to $5.00

LAMINATE

ADVANTAGES. Available in many looks from hardwood to stone and ceramic, laminate flooring is similar to countertop laminate but 20 times stronger. Laminate flooring consists of layers of paper impregnated with resins and compressed into a wear-resistant composite on top of a synthetic backing. It can be laid, or "floated," over an existing floor without being glued to the surface. A floating floor is easy to install using a tongue-and-groove system. When installed properly, it creates a single unit impervious to normal household spills and wear. Costs range from inexpensive for glueless laminates to moderate for higher-end and professionally installed laminates.

DISADVANTAGES. Early products had a tendency to chip or delaminate and were not the best choice near water. Because the floor is floated, it can sound a bit hollow. Underlayments of padding are needed to deaden the sound. Laminate flooring cannot be refinished.

EXPECTED LIFESPAN. 10 to 25 years

MOST APPROPRIATE LOCATIONS. Kitchens, baths, work areas, playrooms

APPROXIMATE COST PER SQUARE FOOT. $2.00 to $5.00

CARPETING

ADVANTAGES. Carpeting cushions feet, provides firm traction, and helps deaden sound. It's especially useful to define smaller areas within multiuse layouts or master suites. New tightly woven commercial products are making carpeting more practical. Like resilient flooring, carpeting is available in an array of styles and materials, with prices that vary widely.

DISADVANTAGES. Usually, the more elaborate the material and weave, the greater the problems from moisture absorption, staining, and mildew. Carpeting used in moisture-prone areas should be short-pile and unsculptured, preferably fabricated of nylon or other synthetics; these are washable and hold up better in moist conditions.

EXPECTED LIFESPAN. 10 to 15 years

MOST APPROPRIATE LOCATIONS. Living rooms, bedrooms, playrooms

APPROXIMATE COST PER SQUARE FOOT. $.50 to $5.00

SPECIALTY

ADVANTAGES. For the most part, concrete, leather, and steel have proven their durability in both commercial and industrial applications and are surprisingly malleable in design. A great variety of colors and patterns can be stamped or embedded into concrete. Leather flooring can be sculpted into unique forms. A grated steel floor allows for air flow, which could be beneficial in many areas.

DISADVANTAGES. While leather maintains great acoustics, a material such as steel does not. Leather requires frequent buffing and waxing. Cost of installation can be high for specialty floors. Every 18 to 36 months, concrete installations should be inspected, cleaned, and resealed as required by volume and intensity of traffic. All these materials require a forward-thinking flooring professional.

EXPECTED LIFESPAN.
- Concrete: Lifetime
- Leather: 15 to 25 years
- Steel: Lifetime, with care

MOST APPROPRIATE LOCATIONS.
- Concrete: Kitchens, baths
- Leather: Dens, home offices
- Steel: Kitchens, work areas

APPROXIMATE COST PER SQUARE FOOT.
- Concrete: $5.00 to $7.00
- Leather: $30.00 to $35.00
- Steel: $15.00 to $25.00

Narrowing the field

There is a flooring material for every location, be it wet, highly trafficked, or noisy. You'll want to consider what you need in a floor before you make a choice. Sometimes a material can be adapted to an environment, but that will increase the costs. Most often the best choice for flooring is the material that meets all your needs.

LOCATION, LOCATION, LOCATION. One of the most important factors to consider is location. Where is your flooring going? How frequently will it be used? Who will be spending most of their time in that room? Floors need to be tailored to the people who use them. A family room should be examined differently than a bedroom, and a family bathroom needs a more hardworking floor than a powder room for guests. Also consider the furniture and other objects that will be used in the room. The wheels of a rolling chair in a home office, for instance, could damage the floor if it's not durable enough for that type of wear.

SAFETY. If your household includes children, the elderly, or a handicapped person, you will want to choose a flooring that accommodates a range of individual preferences and abilities. Here are some factors that affect the safety of a floor.

SLIP RESISTANCE. You may want to look into slip-resistant flooring or finishes. A number of flooring materials feature slip-resistant qualities built right into their design. Naturally, carpeting and vinyl are more slip resistant than stone and tile. And a roughly finished stone is more slip resistant than a highly polished one. On the other hand, ceramic tiles vary in slip resistance and are rated by a coefficient of friction (COF) (see page 107 for more information on COF).

TRAFFIC PATTERNS. Think about how many family members and friends walk in and out of the room to be refloored. Each type of

Sheet vinyl flooring is a natural choice for a kitchen. It's affordable, easy to install, soft underfoot, easy to clean, and it comes in a wider range of colors and designs than ever before.

flooring is rated for durability, usually by its affiliated trade association (the Tile Institute of America or the Southern Pine Council, to name two). You'll want to match the ratings to your own flooring requirements. Also, take note of traffic patterns. How do people cross the room? You may consider installing stronger materials to parallel the foot traffic. With some materials, a designer can plan a floor so a stronger path is incorporated in the overall design of the floor.

SOUND REDUCTION. The advent of in-home entertainment systems has increased the need for sound reduction and better acoustics. If the room you are reflooring will be used for home entertainment, you can add a layer of cork, rubber, or acoustic flooring beneath the floor. These underlayments isolate and absorb sound and can be especially helpful in reducing it in a hallway or from a second floor. They also soften the tone of footsteps on laminate floors.

Abundant light in this living room puts a spotlight on a luxurious floor made from hardwood planks and cork tiles. The grid on the floor is echoed in the mullions of the French doors.

WARMING YOUR TOES

In-floor, or "radiant," heating might seem like a modern indulgence, but the Romans enjoyed the comfort of warm floors long ago. With an in-floor heating system, the entire floor functions as a silent oversized radiator. And it's clean—no air passes through ducts or fins before reaching the room. The room heats up from the bottom up, warming the feet and body first. The bonus? Not only will your toes appreciate radiant heating, but your wallet will too. A radiant system can save at least 25 percent of your energy costs, and it can run on a variety of energy sources.

Currently the two most common types of radiant heating are hydronic and electric. Hydronic radiant floor systems pump heated water from a boiler through polyethylene, rubber, or copper tubing laid in a pattern underneath the floor. The temperature in each room is controlled by regulating the flow of hot water through the tubing.

Electric in-floor heating systems are made of heat-resistant wire that serpentines over a supporting material. Manufacturers offer rolls and mats of these wires in different sizes to fit the shape of each room. Both types of radiant-heat flooring are typically heated to 85 degrees Fahrenheit.

Radiant heating can be installed under all types of floors, although some materials perform better than others. Check with the manufacturer of your radiant heating system for material guidelines. Installing a radiant floor can easily add more than $5 per square foot to the price of your flooring project. However, if you amortize the energy cost savings, it could prove well worth it. A radiant heating system usually pays for itself in about six years.

Do you like the look of a stone floor but don't have the subfloor to support it? Here the look of stone tiles has been replicated in laminate flooring in a kitchen. It looks impressive, cleans up well, and is comfortable underfoot.

LIFE SPAN OF MATERIALS. A number of factors contribute to the life expectancy of flooring materials, including the quality of installation and the level of maintenance during use. A general rule of thumb: Flooring made of natural materials, such as wood or stone, lasts longer than synthetic flooring, such as vinyl. For instance, oak and pine flooring last as long as the home; marble usually lasts beyond the lifetime of the home; and vinyl tiles and vinyl sheet flooring last an average of 20 to 30 years.

Most floors are meant to take a beating with constant use, but if you have children or pets, you'll want to choose flooring that can withstand scratches, spills, and dropped toys to stay good-looking as well as safe.

Consider how long you'll want your flooring to last and compare that to your budget. It may be cost-effective to install flooring that will endure 50 years, rather than using a less-expensive flooring material that will need to be replaced every 10 years. However, if you like change or plan on moving in the near future, you can choose an attractive but inexpensive flooring that you'll be able to change on whim or leave behind if necessary.

INDOOR AIR QUALITY. Indoor air pollution can damage health just as outdoor air pollution does. Air quality has become an issue in relation to flooring because of the adhesives used for installation and claims that certain flooring materials emit chemicals or volatile organic compounds (VOCs) into the air. As a result, low-emitting adhesives are now available that greatly reduce overall installation emissions. They perform as well as their predecessors while adhering to EPA guidelines for improved air quality; ask your installer to use them. You should also be certain that you ventilate your home well during the installation and for at least 48 to 72 hours after. Presently, no floor covering materials are VOC-free; all contain some amount of VOCs for effective performance.

MAINTENANCE. Long after your flooring has been installed, it will continue to need your attention. Depending on the type of flooring you choose, that attention could be minimal or intensive. Know yourself and what routine or periodic maintenance you're willing and able to accept. A leather floor requires buffing every few weeks, a laminate floor needs just a quick wipe with a damp mop, and some wood floors need periodic waxing. Usually the person who purchases the flooring is the one who will clean it. If that's not the case, make sure whoever will be cleaning your floor knows what maintenance is required.

It's also important to recognize that some materials, such as stone and concrete, weather with time. Some people enjoy seeing their floors age gracefully. Others prefer their flooring to remain shiny and new-looking. Take care to choose flooring that suits your preference.

A FLOORING QUESTIONNAIRE

If you've decided you want to redo that floor, it's a good idea to get all your thoughts down on paper before you start rolling up the rugs. This questionnaire can help you analyze your current flooring situation and point you toward ideas for your new floor. Write your answers on a separate sheet of paper, and take that paper with you when meeting with architects, designers, or showroom personnel. The better prepared you are, the smoother the project will go.

1. Why do you want to change the floor? Does it need to be more hardworking? More glamorous?

2. What material(s) would you like to use? Have you considered both traditional and newer materials?

3. How much square footage will be refloored? Does it invlove more than one room?

4. Where is the floor located? In a public or private space?

5. Will moisture be an issue?

7. What is the traffic pattern in the room? Do you have children? Pets?

8. What is your budget?

9. What material covers the floor now? Can it be removed easily?

10. Is the existing subfloor structurally sound?

11. How long do you expect the new floor to last? Do you plan to replace it again?

12. When do you need the floor finished? What is your time framework?

13. For how long can you manage without the new floor?

14. Where are the transitions into other rooms? Are there stairs?

15. What kind of heat do you have? Radiant? Forced air? Baseboard?

16. Will you need outlets and GFIs installed in the floor? Where?

17. Have you considered accessibility and handicap issues?

18. Does anyone in your household suffer from allergies?

19. How will sound in the room be affected by a change in the flooring material?

20. What's your style? Country? Contemporary? Traditional? Eclectic?

21. Do you prefer neutral, bright, or pastel colors?

22. Do you prefer matte or polished finishes? Or a combination?

23. Do you like patterns? Geometrics? Florals? Animal prints?

24. What kind of base trim are you thinking about?

25. How often do you expect to clean and maintain the floor?

designing your floor

WHILE CONSIDERING *the type of flooring material you want, you'll find you have a few other decisions to make as well. What kind of texture do you prefer? Have you thought of mixing different kinds of flooring? Is the size of your flooring pattern in scale with the dimensions of your room? How will the flooring be laid? Here are some basic design concepts for you to consider. Remember, these are helpful guidelines, not set-in-stone rules.*

BELOW: Pattern takes the ordinary and turns it into the extraordinary. A plain hardwood floor is stained with a sunburst pattern to create a unique focal point in a home office. A urethane coating safely seals the pattern.

OPPOSITE: A black-and-white checked ceramic tile floor inspires the overall design of a spunky bathroom. The floor holds the room's busiest mix of pattern, while a more subtle pattern is used at eye level.

Focus or backdrop?

Your new floor will literally underscore the design of the room in which it sits, as well as the adjacent rooms. It should be harmonious with its surroundings while it performs its crucial task of providing a firm foundation to stand on.

You'll be living with your floor every day. Do you want it to be the first thing noticed in the room, or would you prefer it to be a quiet backdrop? Whether focus or backdrop, your

flooring should complement the décor of the room. If you haven't begun to decorate the room, the flooring will serve as a blank canvas. In fact, many people select their flooring first because it covers such a large expanse. It's a lot easier to decide on your flooring and then coordinate the decorative elements, furnishings, and window treatments in the room around the flooring material and style.

Public and private spaces

You'll make different decisions about the new flooring depending on whether it is going into a public area of the house or into a private space. You may want to make the biggest flooring statement in rooms that are frequented by guests. A center medallion of stone or inlaid wood placed in your home's entrance foyer, for example, will serve as a welcome greeting. Placing such a design in a bedroom or in a room where it might be partially covered by furniture would lessen its impact.

In private rooms you'll want to make design choices based on comfort and safety. Thick carpeting may give you the luxurious feel you would like in a master bedroom, while for safety

reasons the choice for the floor in a family bathroom might be slip-resistant tiles.

Elements of design

Designing a room is a way of giving it personality and a look that best expresses your lifestyle. If that sounds daunting, you can break the design down into its components, like style, scale, texture, and those extras that add glamour. Look at each element separately to help you decide how it will affect your flooring choice.

STYLE. The flooring you choose should reflect the style of your house, whether it's contemporary, country, colonial, or eclectic, as well as your personal style. Hardwood floors are a good choice in a turn-of-the-century kitchen, for example, while laminate would work well in a contemporary family room. And slate could be

stunning as it leads guests from a modern foyer right into the great room. Regional design also comes into play. In a southwestern-style home, you might consider terra-cotta tiles for the floor. In an Old World–style villa, handpainted Italian floor tiles might punctuate a dining room.

SCALE. A rule of thumb says oversized flooring belongs in large rooms and small-scale flooring belongs in small rooms. Yet breaking this rule may help you get the look you want. Scale is an important but negotiable element in floor design; it really depends on the room and its environment. In a large room that is bright and airy, it could be fun to install a whimsical mosaic floor. A small bathroom with an oversized checkerboard floor can be effective. One rule that does hold true is that a lengthwise floor pattern adds depth to a room, while a pattern

A roomy master bath with a hardwood floor called for softness both visually and underfoot. A velvety area rug provides the comfort factor. Elegant floral elements are custom-sculpted into the carpet's cut-pile construction.

running the width of a room makes it look shorter and wider.

TEXTURE. A variety of textures adds interest to a room. In flooring, texture can be expressed through glazes and finishes. These finishes can even be combined on one floor for dramatic effect. Some tiles today feature varying textures on the same tile, as if the tile, once polished, had been worn down by time in random places. Stone can be honed, tumbled, or polished for varied appeal. And carpets also offer a choice of texture: closed or cut loops, sheared or carved pile. Looped Berber-style carpeting is one of the most popular carpet textures.

DESIGN EXTRAS. Each type of flooring material comes with its own set of coordinating design accoutrements. Borders, medallions, and inlays now come premade for wood, tile, and stone floors. And the grout that lies between stone or ceramic tiles is very much a design element. Grout joints can be narrow or wide, plain or colored, depending on the look you want.

A woven wool carpet, inspired by sisal carpeting, is used two ways in one home. In the living/dining area, the carpet is laid wall to wall; in the adjacent foyer, it serves as an area rug on a hardwood floor.

They don't make it like they used to. There are times when only reclaimed lumber will achieve the right effect in a room. In the case of this great room, the vintage flooring came from the same source as the beams in this woodsy home.

Design elements can be used to break up the expanse of a large floor, to highlight a focal point, or to define one area of a room. In a multipurpose room, a good design plan can use different types of floor covering to effectively define two or more areas in a single space. For instance, porcelain tile can emphasize the dining area of a carpeted great room, and leather flooring can underscore a home office nestled in a bedroom suite.

MIXED MEDIA. Playing with a variety of materials is a designer's dream. It fosters creativity and allows for infinite design options. Wood can be paired with stone. Ceramic tile can be paired with metal. And concrete flooring can look very sophisticated when embedded with small stones or fossils.

The main concern with a mixed-media floor is how to clean it. Typically, you clean according to the material requiring the most care. Discuss the questions unique to your situation with your flooring professional.

Keeping a visual flow

You'll want visual harmony in your floor so that, in spite of physical interruptions or obstacles like furniture, your eyes will be able to gaze easily across the new floor. Take a look at each of the places where there may be such an interruption and plan for it.

TRANSITIONS AND JUNCTIONS. Think about places where the floor meets the walls, the junction between different types of flooring, and the transition from room to room or level to level. How would you like to finish these edges: Will you choose a baseboard molding to edge the perimeter of the floor? Will you have tile run up the toe-kick of your kitchen cabinets? Will you want a marble saddle to make the transition from your wood floor to a marble floor? Or do you prefer all the flooring—carpet, wood, and stone—to be on a level plane? This can be done, but it requires a bit of preplanning with your contractor.

STAIRS. If you have a staircase that is affected by your flooring project, you'll want to work it into the theme of your floor. Trimming the risers with the same material as the floor will help to coordinate the stairs with the room. It will also make the stairway safer by providing a visual cue for the elevation.

GRILLES, REGISTERS, AND OUTLETS. Not usually thought of as attractive, grilles, registers, and outlets perform necessary functions in your home. Grilles and registers allow heat to come into a room. New designs now available include unique cutwork patterns as well as colors and materials that coordinate with your new floor.

In-floor outlets allow for more flexibility in the arrangement of furniture. You can place a lamp next to a sofa in the middle of a living room, for example, without having an electrical cord running all the way across the floor to a wall outlet. You'll need to plan ahead and decide where you would like your in-floor outlets to go.

PICK YOUR PATTERN

Most flooring that is composed of squares or pavers can be laid out in a number of ways. Choosing the right pattern for your floor can have a strong impact on its final design. A simple turn or shift of a square will liven up even the most basic flooring. Patterns can also be used to direct the eye to a room's focal point.

Typically, larger patterns are reserved for large rooms and smaller patterns for smaller rooms. As you're deciding what you want, keep in mind that large patterns don't always make a room look smaller. Sometimes they actually open up a room, while small patterns, such as tiny checkerboards, make a space feel cozier.

While choosing your floor, consider other patterns in the room. If your walls are covered in large-scale stripes, you may want your floor to be more subtle. A simple pattern can also help tie together large spaces and produce a feeling of calm.

These patterns are commonly found in flooring design. They each feature countless variations on their theme.

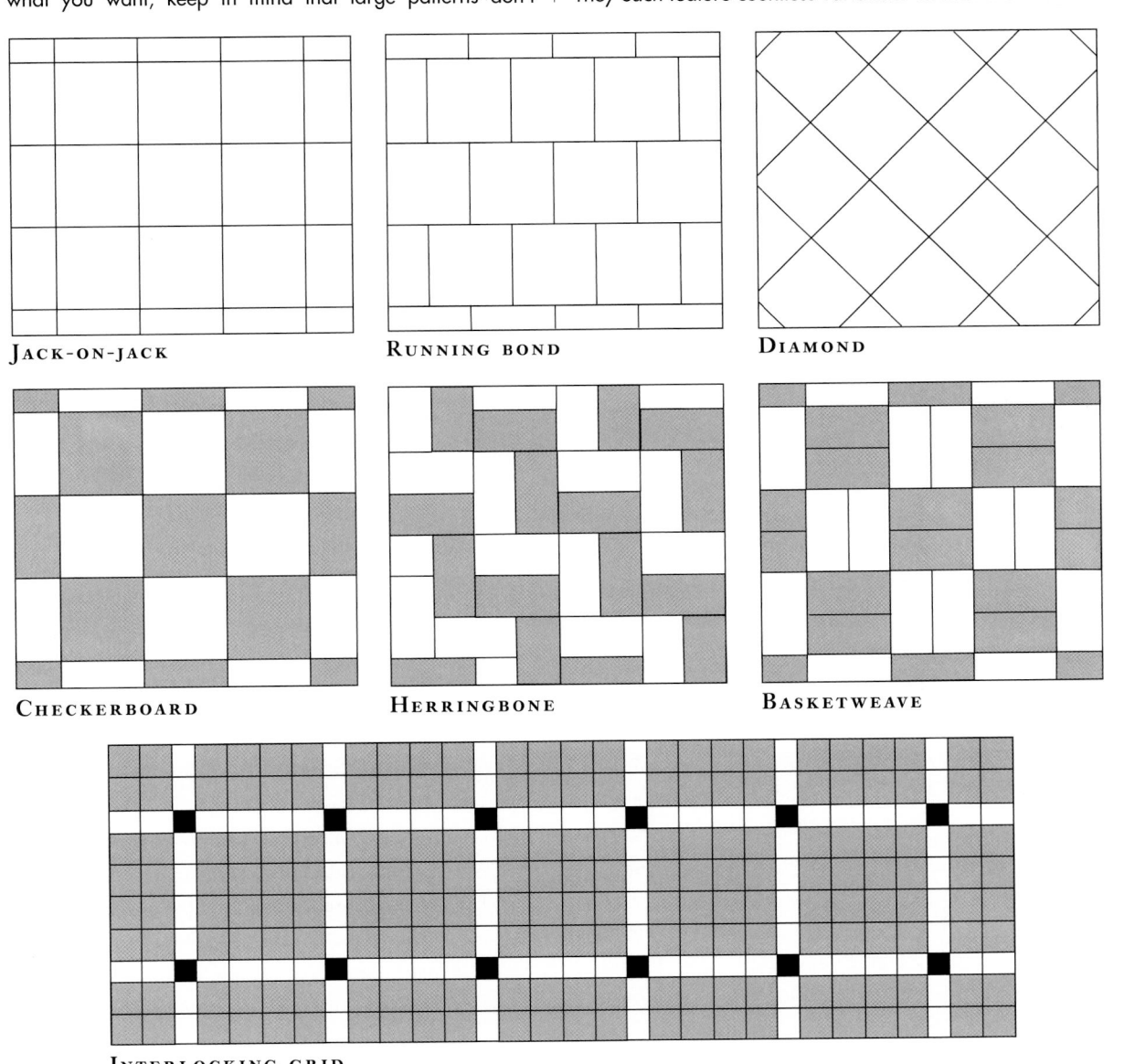

JACK-ON-JACK

RUNNING BOND

DIAMOND

CHECKERBOARD

HERRINGBONE

BASKETWEAVE

INTERLOCKING GRID

gearing up

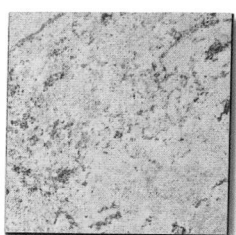

INSTALLING A NEW FLOOR *can be a simple one-day task or a major home improvement. Before you begin, be aware of what your project entails. Your home will be disrupted for a while, so look at a variety of options and ask lots of questions. Survey showrooms and home centers and interview flooring professionals. And don't hesitate to ask for help when you need it.*

Be prepared

A well-stocked flooring showroom or a large home center can be overwhelming in the sheer number of choices it offers, so it's best to do some homework before you visit one. You'll be better able to consider a showroom's professional recommendations and evaluate the choices if you have some ideas in mind.

GATHER YOUR IDEAS. Your inspirations can come from a variety of places. Browse through magazines and books (like this one) and print on-line images. If you're redoing a great room floor, don't confine yourself to finding great room pictures. Take a look at images of other rooms as well. Who knows? You might find the perfect great room floor in a master bathroom photo. For color ideas, gather paint chips, swatches from fabrics used in the room, or favorite vacation snapshots. Create a scrapbook of possibilities and include rough measurements of the room and an outline of your floor. Make note of where light enters the room and where adjoining rooms exist. Take the scrapbook and your notes with you on your showroom outings.

MONEY-SAVING TIPS. Stretch your dollars as far as they will go. There are lots of ways to

get a great-looking floor on a limited budget. Here are some hints:

■ Choose a less expensive material that emulates a costlier one.

■ Work with an inexpensive material like resilient flooring and lay it out in an interesting pattern.

■ Have a local artist detail your wood flooring with faux techniques to look like inlaid mahogany.

■ Use costlier stones and tiles as a border or accents in a field of stock tile.

■ Watch for flooring closeouts or shop for seconds. Some retailers keep their closeouts and seconds available in a separate room.

Where to go

Flooring can be purchased from a variety of sources. Distributors usually specialize in one type of product. Tile and stone distributors are the most familiar. Floor-covering retailers carry a range of different types of flooring materials. Home centers also offer a broad range of materials, often at good prices. Visit several places and shop where you feel comfortable. Imported materials used to take a long time to ship, but that's not so true today because large distributors often maintain a warehouse.

Planning ahead counts for a lot. Once you have decided on the design and layout, you'll find that installing a cork floor like the one shown opposite is a relatively speedy peel-and-stick or glue-down process.

You can call on professionals to help you plan creatively. One inspired designer specified a contrasting shade of ceramic tile to form a "carpet" beneath a dining table. The inset in the floor coordinates with the wall tile.

Ask your flooring installer for samples. Most contractors carry a limited number of samples for you to peruse at home. Requesting flooring samples from retailers is a good idea too. You may be charged a small fee, but you'll get to view the sample in its destined environment.

Need help?

For help in installing flooring, you'll want to contact an architect, interior designer, or installer. Ask friends and family for referrals. Retailers can also refer you to flooring professionals; in fact, larger retailers often subcontract installations. Architects can help you analyze your particular needs and find solutions to tricky problems. Designers are more attuned to style and know about the latest materials.

It's a good idea to get about three estimates for your floor. Ask for references and check to

see if the contractor is licensed to perform the intended work. Estimates should include all subfloor preparation, all installation costs, the removal of the existing flooring, the moving of furniture and appliances, and all the necessary flooring materials.

Practical matters

Once you've set a date for installing your new floor, be sure you know when and where your materials will be arriving. In order to acclimate to new surroundings, your flooring material may need to sit in your home for a while before the job begins. Let your contractor know where materials should be left. Stone may simply be left in your driveway, but wood flooring will need to be stored inside and kept dry.

Installing a floor often takes longer than you think. That can be especially frustrating if you're getting your home ready for a holiday or family event. Plan ahead and allow the right amount of time for the floor to settle in its new surroundings before you have a house full of guests. The grout and mortar in a new tile floor require curing time. New carpeting has an odor that needs time to fade a bit.

REMOVING YOUR OLD FLOOR. You don't always need to remove your existing flooring. However, if it is truly in bad shape or if adding a new floor on top of it will increase the height of your flooring significantly or will block in appliances, you'll want to remove it.

If the existing floor is resilient and manufactured before 1986, it should be tested for asbestos at a private laboratory. A positive test result means you have to take special precautions to remove the material safely. Check with your local Environmental Protection Agency office. If you choose not to remove the resilient flooring, you can lay most types of flooring right over it.

SUBFLOORS. Before you visit flooring retailers, see if you can tell what's underneath your existing floor. Your contractor will also take a look. Make sure the subfloor is in good condition. This is not the place to skimp. Your flooring installation will only be as good as the subfloor underneath it. A springy or sagging floor is not a good sign. An imperfect subfloor can cause cracked ceramic tiles or allow for moisture to gather, which causes wood planks to cup and joists to squeak. Serious structural problems call for further expertise.

WHEN TO REFINISH. All types of flooring can be patched, repaired, or refinished. Perhaps your old floor just needs sprucing up. A new color grout for a tiled floor? A different finish for a wood floor? If the imperfections on your wood floor are shallow, it can be stripped and given a fresh finish rather than sanded. If your floor has heavier damage and does need to be sanded, sanding will remove only a small percentage of the depth, so you can safely resand a solid wood floor every 15 to 20 years.

TIME AND SPACE

Numbers are important in replacing flooring, both to determine the amount of space you'll be covering and to estimate the length of time you'll need to allow to complete the job.

The timing of your project will depend on the material you choose. A resilient, laminate, or carpeted floor can be installed in less than one day, plus 24 hours for glues and adhesives to set. A tile, stone, or wood floor will take longer and could require an extra three to four days for finishing, sealing, curing, and drying. In addition, leveling out an imperfect subfloor can add even more time, depending on the extent of the work.

To determine how much flooring you'll need, measure the longest length and the widest width of your room. Divide odd-shaped rooms, and figure each section separately. Ceramic tile, stone, resilient tile, wood, and laminate are measured by the square foot. Sheets of resilient flooring and carpeting are measured by the square yard. For these materials, measure in square feet and divide by 9 to determine square yardage. For good measure, on all materials add 10 percent to allow for errors and pattern matching. You'll also want to keep some extra materials on hand for future repairs.

GREAT FLOOR IDEAS

Now **that** you've explored your options, it's time to be inspired! In this chapter you'll find that ideas for great floors are many and varied. As you start your search, you'll come across floors that you think are terrific. You can mark those photographs and then go back later to pare down your favorites. As you revisit the photographs, you'll begin to discover your flooring preferences. **Once you've narrowed** down your choices, ask yourself some questions about each one. Is it practical for your lifestyle? Will it fit in with the décor of your home? Be sure to share these flooring photographs with your designer or contractor. The more they see what you like, the more likely you'll get the floor you want. Take your time and consider your choices carefully. **Making the right choice** for your home is a big decision. Your new floor needs to be both practical and beautiful to be a real success!

tile

THE APPEAL OF ceramic tile cannot be understated. Encompassing ceramic, porcelain, quarry tile, and mosaics, ceramic tile in all its shapes and forms presents one of the widest ranges of flooring available in any one category. In addition, glistening glass tiles, though technically not ceramic, appear in this chapter. Some floors feature the timeless look of tile set with wide grout lines, as in popular terra-cotta tile floors, while other floors, such as those with large-format porcelain tiles set with tight or no-grout joints, provide a seamless appearance. Today ceramic tile has become a virtual chameleon and has been designed to mimic other materials, most notably replicating large slabs of marble or granite. Even photographic images are finding their way onto tiles. How about photos of water on the floor of a guest bathroom? Or lush green grass tiles for a garden room?

Another aspect of ceramic tile that might surprise you is its use throughout the house. On these pages you will see ceramic tile flooring move outside the kitchen and bath into other areas of the home. Many American designers are taking their cue from European homes, which often use ceramic tile flooring in living rooms and bedrooms. The concept works exceptionally well in homes with open floor plans or loftlike spaces where you can see several rooms from one vantage point.

Ceramic tile can be new and exciting, as well as old and traditional. You may be inspired by a tile idea that you never thought of before or become enamored with a classic tiled floor.

Unusually shaped and creatively set ceramic mosaics form a rug design in the center of a mosaic-tiled room. The "rug" provides color, while the rest of the floor remains neutral.

Contrasting with bright yellow walls, a highly polished black-and-white porcelain checkerboard floor is an unexpected greeting for visitors to a traditional home. Tightly butted joints let the glossy look continue uninterrupted through the hallway.

Sturdy porcelain tiles mimic the texture and shadings of stone on the floor of a cozy sitting room. An "area rug" created with tiles placed on the diagonal and finished with a border of smaller tiles covers the main activity center of the room.

Simple, timeless squares of ceramic tile in neutral shades of gray and taupe are randomly arranged on the floor of a sitting alcove. Not only are the tile shades mixed, but the tiles themselves are set off-center from one another.

A bisque-colored ceramic tile floor complements a large, sunny kitchen. The light color is repeated in the wall tiles covering the kitchen's backsplash.

Set on an angle and featuring a very traditional grout line, gray ceramic tile covers the floor of a kitchen and dining area. The lines of the floor lead directly to an outdoor patio.

Ceramic tile squares patterned to look like stone run parallel to the work island in a contemporary kitchen. Narrow joints and shading that blends with the kitchen cabinetry contribute to the room's monochromatic design.

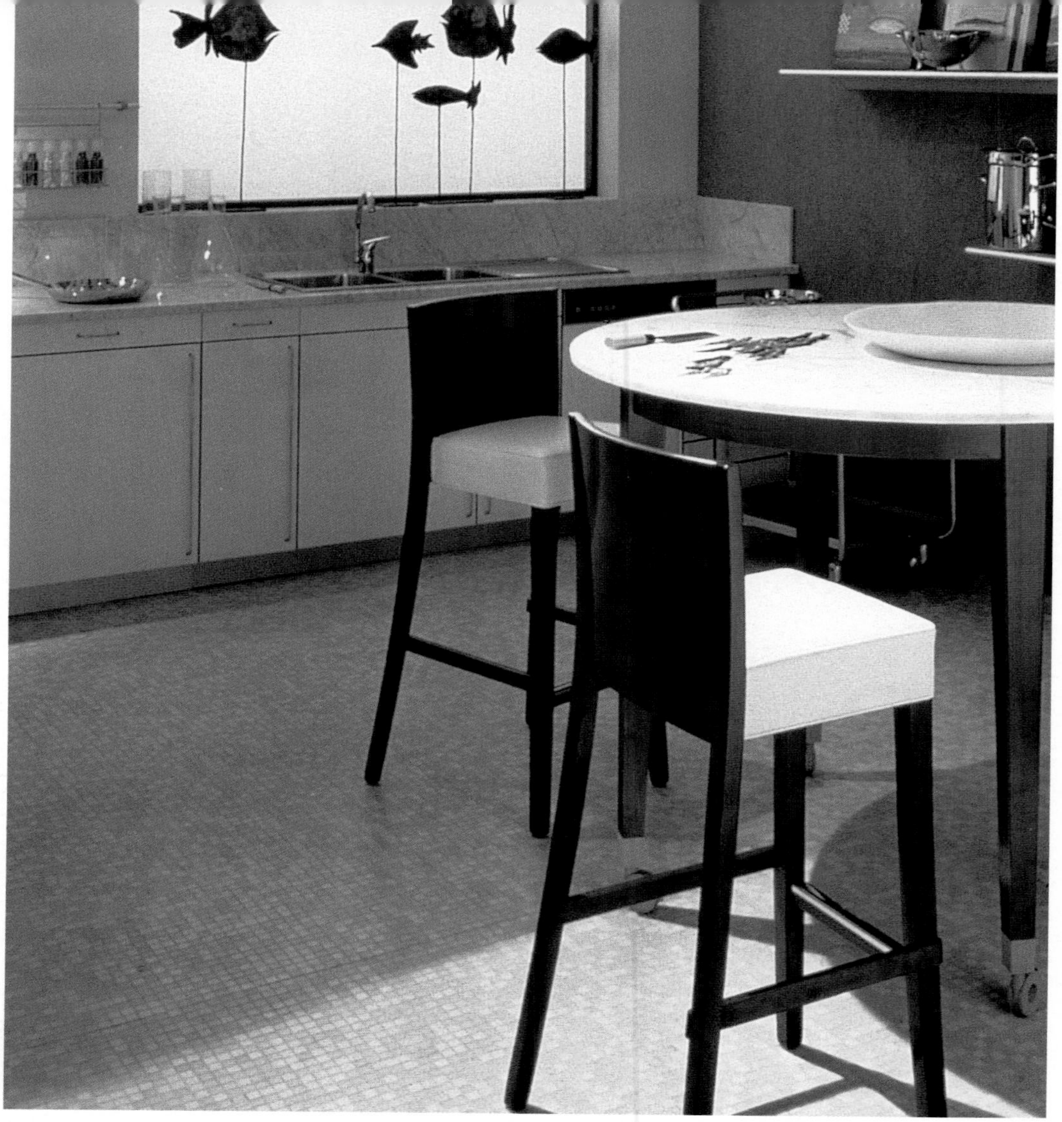

Not typically thought
of for expansive
open spaces today,
translucent glass mosaic
tiles on the floor bring
an air of serenity to
a busy eat-in kitchen.
The floor's soft neutral
shades look custom-
made but were chosen
from standard glass
mosaic colors.

Traditional porcelain
mosaic tiles are set in a
classic interlocking grid
pattern on this kitchen
floor. The use of black
tiles at each intersection
visually breaks up the
predominant use of
white in the room.

Colorful glass mosaic
tiles replicate a vintage
Persian carpet complete
with fringe. The carpet
was prefabricated
for easy installation
and set in a frame
of neutral-colored
oversized stone tiles
that allow the "carpet"
to take center stage.

*Glass mosaics
cover virtually all
the surfaces in a
contemporary master
bath. Visually opening
up the narrow space,
the mosaics run from
floor to ceiling and
bath to shower,
interrupted only by
a vanity mirror and
picture window.*

*A combination of
square and rectangular
ceramic tiles forms an
interlocking grid on
the floor of an elegant
master bath. Matching
tiles run up the wall
and outfit the shower,
while copper-colored
marble mosaics
accenting the floor
grid are repeated on
the backsplash.*

*Handcrafted ceramic
leaves are set free-form
within a border and
field of preset pebble
mosaic tiles to create a
focal point in a guest
bath. The wide mortar
joints and deep texture
provide some slip
resistance to bathers
stepping out of the tub.*

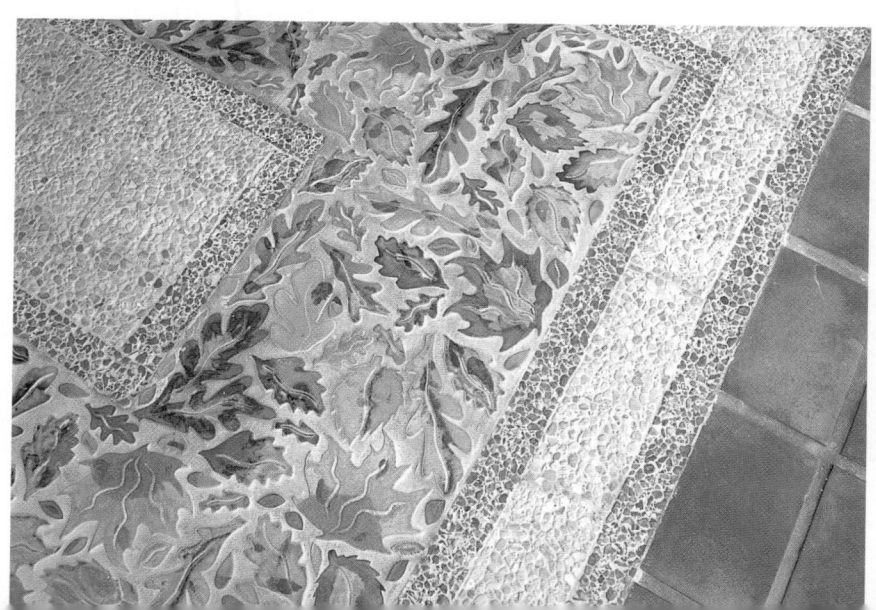

Reproduced on large-format ceramic tiles, modular images of manhole covers, crosswalks, and asphalt combine to create a vivid urban streetscape inside a novel bath. The colorful crosswalk tiles follow the entire border of the room.

A simple shower floor features images of river rocks photo-transferred onto ceramic tile. The sharp-focus photography used on the tiles brings a sense of depth to the floor. A slightly abrasive surface makes the floor safer when wet.

A field of glazed porcelain mosaics covers the floor and makes the transition into the shower of a half-bath. Small boxes of black mosaics line the perimeter of the room and run up the center of the shower. A painted wood baseboard completes the floor, and simple black-and-white accessories accentuate the design.

Pillowed terra-cotta flooring paired with tall paned windows makes a dining room look like a garden room. Hand-molded ceramic accent tiles are inset throughout the diagonally set floor, while multiple intersecting lines call attention away from the room's baseboard heating.

Obtuse angles of the cabinetry in an Old World kitchen called for uniquely shaped tiles. A combination of octagonal and square terra-cotta floor tiles complements the space, while decorative glazed accent tiles provide contrast.

Sealed terra-cotta tiles cover the floor of a small guest bedroom, more often used as a den. The randomly mixed colors of the tiles can be attributed to the ceramic clay's natural unglazed state. A wide grout line filled with neutral mortar emphasizes the handcrafted appeal.

stone

NATURAL STONE is among the oldest types of flooring available. Stone can be imported from exotic faraway places or quarried from your own backyard, if you're lucky enough to have such an indigenous treasure. The following pages are filled with fabulous examples, both traditional and contemporary, of granite, limestone, marble, flagstone, and slate from both near and far. If there is an overriding theme, it's that most of the stone floors shown here embody a sense of history. Even the whimsical terrazzo floors you'll see have origins that can be traced back centuries, when masons would actually hand-place chips of marble and other stones into mortar to form a terrazzo slab.

These floors belong in their environments. The distinguishing characteristic of a stone floor—whether it's the depth of color in a highly polished glamorous marble or the softly rounded edges of an earthy limestone—should fit within the room. The floor should complement its surroundings and provide foundation, but it should not overpower or compete.

Take note as you look at various types of stone flooring. What is it about these floors that engages you? Is it the charm of weathered and tumbled edges that you like? Or is it the sleekness of highly polished slabs with undetectable joints? What colors interest you? You might begin your search with a strong predisposition for a uniform pattern of granite and end up falling in love with a variegated red slate. Keep your mind open and consider the options.

Tightly jointed squares of polished white Carrara marble carry the serene vintage feel of a 1930s-style bathroom. A simple baseboard of painted wood molding neatly finishes the outer edges of the floor.

Insets of unglazed terra-cotta mosaics repeat the theme of a tiled wall frieze across a yellow marble floor. A geometric strip of the marble tile marks the transition into an adjacent room, where solid terra-cotta insets take the place of the mosaics.

Speckled granite tiles contrast with a living room's sleek white marble fireplace. Complemented by black grout lines, the speckled pattern camouflages footprints and dust, letting the homeowners enjoy the beauty of the room's monochromatic design.

A black-and-white granite floor runs all the way through a contemporary loft-style space, cutting across expansive living, dining, and entertaining areas. Tightly butted slabs give the appearance of a seamless floor, while geometric area rugs and partitioning walls provide definition and warmth.

Varying patchworks of tumbled limestone emerge as a hallway progresses from one room to the next. A limestone medallion defines the library, while diagonally set squares lead into a home office. Borders of highly polished striated marble frame each section.

Tumbled limestone tiles set in linear rows softly underscore a simple white kitchen with a touch of color and texture. The floor's white grout lines pick up the white of the cabinets. The gridded floor unites the dining area, the kitchen, and the entry.

Alternating sizes, shapes, and shades of limestone floor tiles carry the eclectic theme of a country kitchen. The earthy tiles and white grout provide a neutral foundation.

Oversized limestone slab flooring in a color called Princess Yellow has been cut to fit the dimensions of a sparely decorated modern living area. The seamless surface enhances the room's open design while anchoring the entire space with subtle tones of color and texture.

Narrow slate tiles finish the whirlpool tub surround in a master bath and also form the room's baseboard. The use of the same material over several surfaces visually opens the space. Interest is achieved by offsetting the placement of tiles on the floor.

A tightly jointed polished limestone floor begins in the open kitchen and runs through a main hallway, helping to create continuity between the work and entertainment areas of the house. Field tiles are set on a diagonal within a border of the same limestone. The limestone is also used for the baseboard.

A very straightforward gray slate floor contrasts with
unfettered light wood cabinetry in a contemporary kitchen.
The room's great dimension is emphasized and pattern is
achieved by the simple use of white grout lines.

Varied shades of slate tiles fill a rustic great room with hues from yellow to purple. A reclaimed oak saddle beneath a pair of French doors creates a warm transition from outside to in, and a bamboo doormat adds visual interest while helping to keep debris from the outdoors to a minimum.

Mixed neutral shades of desert slate tiles run right up to the wood wainscoting in a den, continuing the room's refined Mission style. The floor's tight joints and linear setting further emphasize a restrained quality.

A combination of traditional gray slate and stainless steel cool down a hardworking kitchen and provide surfaces that perform as well as they look. The floor's mix of sizes and patterns adds visual interest where it's least expected and contributes to the geometry of the room.

great floor ideas

Vintage cobblestones were reclaimed for use in a garden-facing kitchen. The offset placement of the stones follows the pattern of the exterior stone and leads the eye into the garden. A row of short cobblestones finishes the outer edge of the floor where it abuts the French doors.

Classic terrazzo tiles enliven the ultramodern look in a master bath. Alternating brown and yellow hues were used to achieve a checkerboard effect that enlivens an otherwise all-white room.

Although each pebble looks as though it were painstakingly hand-laid centuries ago, Arabesque tiles of natural river pebbles, used here in the sunlit foyer of a new home, come preconfigured. Even the mortar is preworked into the tiles.

wood

IT SEEMS AS IF wood floors are everywhere. A maple floor gives warmth to a vintage kitchen; pine blends almost effortlessly into the living room of an older home; an oak floor lends an air of timelessness to the great room in a new home. Deciding on a new wood floor is the first step. You'll want to choose a particular type of wood, then a board size and a finish to get the desired effect from a wood floor. Will it be a deep, rich mahogany that starkly contrasts with white walls, or a lighter honey shade that makes a room cozy? Do you want to recapture the timeworn characteristics and markings that make wood special? Today you can install vintage floors resurrected from former estates or use boards from age-old logs recovered from riverbeds. There are also alternative new woods, such as bamboo, that have been embraced for their sustainable harvests and for the unique elongated patterns found in their planks.

In keeping with the simplicity of a colonial theme, a wide-plank hardwood floor is given a wax finish. The low luster of the floor blends well with the room's trim.

A warm nutmeg stain finishes a white oak strip floor in a comfortable living room. The grain of the wood floor provides an interesting contrast to the carved stone fireplace and decorative iron fire screen. Running parallel to the fireplace, the floor features a floating wood installation.

Wood floors can serve as the ultimate canvas in a room. Beyond their intrinsic color and texture, they can be intricately painted, washed with shades of color, or inset with creative geometrics. They can be the focus of a room or become a backdrop for the furnishings. What should you look for in wood floors? Most important will be your preference for color, but also note the width of the planks that interest you and the texture of the boards. Wood floors look good in every room of the house—which type of wood is up to you.

Wide bleached planks cover the floor of a rustic great room, serving as a light backdrop to heavy furnishings and upholstery. The floor's light color makes the expanse of the floor look even greater, while the wood's random knots add to the appeal of the room's eclectic interior.

Providing a satiny smooth surface against contrasting dark furnishings, clear maple planking in shades of toast covers the floor of a sophisticated modern bedroom. The bed's headboard and the area rug, set perpendicular to the direction of the flooring, place an emphasis on the long planks.

Knotty pine floors in the great room of a log home repeat the
pine used in the construction of the home itself, creating an all-
enveloping natural environment for homeowners who appreciate
the respite of down-home character. The judicious placement of
the furniture leaves visible great expanses of the beautiful floor.

*Alternating hues of
birch flooring run
fluidly through an
open kitchen and
throughout the
common areas of
a contemporary home.
The direction of the
planks follows the path
of the main hallway.*

*Vertical-grain bamboo
strips showing all
the character of exotic
wind-blown grass
enliven the floor of a
sitting area and the
working part of the
kitchen beyond it.
Stone tiles are inset
at the hearth.*

*Flat-grain bamboo
flooring covers the
kitchen area of a great
room with abundant
light. A contrasting
baseboard runs
along the base of the
cabinetry. In the
adjacent living area,
a handsome concrete
floor was poured in
place to the same level
as the bamboo floor.*

Aged wide-plank
hardwoods salvaged
from old warehouses
are strategically mixed
and matched on the
floor of an adobe-style
southwestern living
room. The planks
run at an angle to
the room's overhead
beams, creating a
sweeping effect out to
panoramic views.

A simple combination
of standard hardwood
strip flooring in
contrasting colors
creates a custom look
in a formal dining
room. A wide band of
dark-stained planks
serves as the transition
from dining to living
room, where clear light
wood flooring is used.

In a small dining
room, a floor of
understated clear oak
is accented simply
by a narrow strip
of contrasting wood
along the perimeter of
the room. A painted
white baseboard is
incorporated into
faux wainscoting
rather than blended
with the floor.

In a diminutive sitting area, a parquet floor is installed on a diagonal to the room's walls. A double row of contrasting wood strips outlines the space, while a painted baseboard finishes the floor. A marble slab is used at the hearth.

A subtle parquet floor features a single wide band of contrasting parquet, giving needed line and angularity to a lush bedroom with soft, rounded forms. Situated in the center of the room, the band takes on a life of its own, not following the shape of the bed or the room's perimeter.

A border of parquet wood flooring curves around the landing of a main staircase. The mix of woods highlights the shadings of the turn-of-the-century stair banister.

A strategically designed pattern in maple strip wood set
against a background of pine flooring underscores the formal
entrance of a traditional home. The pattern, as wide as the
double entry doors, adds a welcoming brightness to the floor
in this sunlit foyer. The pine flooring continues seamlessly
into the adjacent room.

Undulating lines form a romantic hand-painted border around a dining room table. The sheer stains used to create the effect allow the grain of the flooring to show through and blend with the room's décor.

Faux painting gives an old hardwood floor new life. Rather than install a new floor, the vintage oak floor was hand-painted to look like rich, heavily veined marble. Even border tiles are painted around the edge of the room and the staircase.

In a child's room a painted finish softens hardwood strip flooring. The floor's pattern of interlocking pastel diamonds is charming, yet sophisticated enough to grow with the child. A painted border follows the room's built-in cabinetry.

Lacework from antique linens inspired the intricate hand-painted hardwood floor in a nursery. Coats of gray-blue paint, the only color in the room, were used to cover the floor first. Then a delicate coat of white "lace" was applied.

Vivid blue paint is washed over the hardwood strip flooring of a living room and extends onto the saddles beneath the exterior doors, bringing the eye to the glorious view outside. No surface of the hardwood floor is left untouched by the wash. A slightly raised area of white ceramic tiles forms a semicircle at the hearth.

resilient

RESILIENT FLOORING is a material you can have fun with. Because it is relatively inexpensive, easy to install, and simple to maintain, resilient flooring invites playful design. Imagine creating an amusing checkerboard with basic red and black vinyl tiles in a children's playroom, or livening up a laundry room with vividly speckled vinyl sheeting. Or imagine mixing varying shades and sizes of stone-colored vinyl in an entryway. The new stone designs in vinyl look surprisingly authentic, as do some of the wood-patterned vinyls.

Although vinyl comes first to mind, resilient flooring encompasses a range of malleable materials—vinyl, linoleum, cork, and rubber—each with its own unique characteristics. Linoleum can take on a retro look that would be wonderful in a renovated mid-century kitchen, or it can be sophisticated enough for use in a living room. Cork can add a touch of nature while helping to mute sound in a media room rich with technology or in a kid's playroom.

A vividly striped linoleum runner that follows the length of an entry hall contrasts starkly with the hall's cool gray concrete surface. Used in place of carpeting, linoleum provides a colorfast covering for the southern-exposed space.

Green linoleum provides a hard-working surface for three well-used rooms: a living/dining area, a galley kitchen, and a laundry room. Whimsical linoleum cutouts capture the color of each area as the floor pattern ebbs and flows, defining each room yet emphasizing the continuity of the space.

Rubber flooring has a contemporary look and holds up to rugged use.

It's a given that all resilient flooring is comfortable underfoot. But resilients are also available in the broadest spectrum of colors of any flooring material, which leads to creative ways to use them. Take a look at the range of patterns in each type of resilient flooring, how they're laid out, and how they work visually within a room. From simple mixing and matching of colors to custom inlaid designs, there's a resilient floor for every style and for every room.

Easy-care vinyl sheet flooring in a mosaic pattern that evokes garden paths of long ago brings the outdoors into a sunny family room. The wicker furniture and potted plants further the outdoor look.

Linoleum tiles in soft shades of beige and ecru give an earthly grounding to a starkly modern white living room. Baskets for firewood and plants on the coffee table pick up the natural feel of the floor.

Sheet vinyl that looks like hardwood planking runs wall to
wall in a classically styled living room. The plank pattern
runs across the room toward the focal point on the far wall—
a picturesque window seat. A painted white baseboard
anchors the easy-to-maintain yet warmly inviting flooring.

*Alternating colors
of vinyl tiles in a
traditional kitchen
give the illusion of a
ceramic-tiled floor
complete with grout
lines. An oversized
sculpted baseboard
molding is paired with
the large checkerboard
pattern, which flows
from the kitchen to
the dining area.*

*A play of mixed media
is achieved by the use
of sheet vinyl in a
living room. The floor
looks like artfully
installed hardwood
flooring inset with slate
tiles, an effect that only
a skilled installer
could achieve.*

*Patterned sheet
vinyl in an open
kitchen only looks like
individually laid tiles.
Its sophisticated design
continues the room's
neutral tones but also
adds a texture that
seems to ground
the columned high-
ceilinged space.*

An unanticipated patchwork of brightly colored cork tiles
underscores a frequently used dining room in a landmark home.
For the family who enjoys entertaining, the cork provides a soft
surface underfoot and minimizes the sound of footsteps in the
room. The multicolored tiles provide a springboard for the
simple furnishings, including the large wood trestle table.

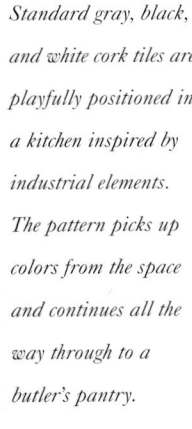

Standard gray, black, and white cork tiles are playfully positioned in a kitchen inspired by industrial elements. The pattern picks up colors from the space and continues all the way through to a butler's pantry.

Cork flooring outfits a stair landing, providing an attractive surface, as well as traction for safe footing. The area is bordered by geometric black-and-white tiles that serve as a guide to the home's other rooms.

laminate

Laminate mimics a vintage wide-plank floor in a turn-of-the-century styled kitchen filled with freestanding appliances. The black-grained pattern of the wide planks leads the eye toward a large window with a garden view.

LAMINATE IS one of the newest types of flooring. Introduced in Sweden as an alternative to hardwood, it became a flooring favorite almost immediately. It's a natural choice when you want to combine goods looks, easy maintenance, and quick installation.

Most laminates replicate wood flooring. But wood-patterned laminate is definitely not one-dimensional. Just like solid wood, wood-patterned laminate comes in a range of styles — from elegant to rustic to contemporary. You can also find precious and exotic woods, like chestnut or teak, emulated in laminate.

Many intricate and sophisticated wood designs, such as weaves and herringbones, are also available in laminate. In real wood such designs would be costly because of the labor-intensive handwork they require. In laminate, however, designs are possible that might not even be considered in wood.

In addition to wood, ceramic- and stone-patterned laminate tiles are also available. Cut into squares rather than planks, these laminates allow for some creative applications. Marble colors can be mixed for innovative checkered floors. Similar colors can be placed on the floor and along the perimeter to create a subtle border. The look of seamless flooring can be created by using laminate tiles in one color, such as a single shade of granite-patterned laminate.

By viewing laminate floors in actual rooms, you'll see how wood and stone patterns and their variations accommodate a variety of styles. Keep an eye out for designs and colors that interest you to help narrow down your choices.

A wall of cheery turquoise cabinets is anchored by a light pine laminate floor. A slim dark molding defines the line where the two meet. The pattern of the narrow laminate planks runs parallel to a main wall, visually expanding the kitchen's width.

Laminate provides a splinter-free, easy-to-maintain surface in a child's nursery. The baby can crawl, drop toys, and spill foods without getting hurt or harming the floor. The molded hardwood baseboard is painted the same color as the room's walls.

Golden bamboo laminate flooring captures the multicultural theme of a family room while providing a neutral background for the room's dark furnishings. The simple flat baseboard molding is stained to match a pair of carved wood doors.

An understated laminate floor runs the depth of a reading nook off a formal living room. Outside the nook the laminate flooring runs diagonally, drawing the eye in. An Oriental carpet softens any echoes in the space and helps keep this home library a quiet place to read.

A natural laminate floor performs well in the highly trafficked entrance and living area off the kitchen of a small apartment. The floor's color anchors the room's splash of lavender-hued walls.

A light wood laminate floor brings color and texture to an otherwise unadorned white kitchen. The grain pattern in the floor hides footprints and spills until they can be swept away.

A cost-effective flooring alternative, laminate emulates a ceramic tile surface in this old-fashioned bath. The modular tile units fit together along simulated "grout lines," giving the look that usually comes only from master craftsmen.

A minimalist bedroom receives its visual interest from an artfully laid laminate floor. The floor's muted shades are defined by a contrasting baseboard. An underlayment of felted material softens the sound of footsteps across the floor.

carpet

THERE'S NO DENYING the warmth and security that a lush carpet can bring to a room. It's the kind of comfort underfoot you want for your family. And if your family includes children, there is no need to be concerned about the high maintenance of carpeting. Today's stain-resistant finishes mean easy care and less worry in choosing carpeting.

On the following pages you will see wall-to-wall carpeting and a range of area rugs. You'll notice that area rugs can work well in certain circumstances. If you have an existing wood floor, you can let the wood show in all its glory from beneath an area rug cut smaller than the room. Or you can use a simple area rug to delineate one area of a floor, like a dining space. In a bedroom suite you may prefer wall-to-wall carpeting. Installing it from the bedroom through the dressing area and into the bathroom means that in the morning your feet never have to touch a cold floor.

Once you've decided whether an area rug or wall-to-wall carpeting is best for your room, take a look at color and weave and fiber. Do you want your carpet to make a statement or create a subtle background? Do you want the look and maintenance of a shag carpet or the easy care of tightly woven level loop? Would you like carpeting made of woven plants and grasses, such as sisal, or traditional wools and familiar manufactured fibers? When you choose carpets as your flooring, you'll have myriad choices in color, texture, and fiber.

Soft lavender carpeting with a velvety cut pile runs wall to wall in a living room, bringing a hint of color to the Asian-style furnishings.

Ceramic tile flooring cleverly frames the white cut-pile carpeting in a highly styled living room. The carpet itself follows the lines of a custom sectional sofa in the room. Painstaking efforts were taken in installing the flooring to assure that the carpet was level with the tile, a look that adds to the luxurious feel of the room.

A cut-and-loop pile creates a textured trellis pattern for wall-to-wall carpeting in a comfortable living room. The carpeting's soft color functions as a neutral that allows for a great deal of flexibility in design.

The natural-color loop pile of a berber carpet blends into a living room by mimicking the nubby texture of the room's sofa, yet it contrasts with its adjacent design elements—the sofa's long silk fringe and the sinuously shaped table legs.

An allover Persian-inspired pattern and an intricate floral border are the hallmarks of this colorful, closely clipped Oriental rug. Not only does the carpet provide a design focus in the foyer; it also protects the wide-plank hardwood floor.

The conversation area of a sunlit blue-and-yellow living room is centered around a floral needlepoint rug with diagonally shaped corners. The rug, designed to echo the patterns in the upholstery, protects the room's hardwood floor under the furniture but does not conceal the wood in the rest of the room.

The words to a familiar childhood nursery rhyme are sculpted into the border of a custom-made area rug for a baby's room. The rug's plush cut pile provides a cushiony platform for baby's first steps.

A charming broadloom carpet designed with primitive childlike imagery covers the floor of a toddler's playroom. The dense short-loop pile allows the carpet's vivid colors to pop and provides an easy-to-clean surface.

An imaginative area rug in a home office gives the illusion of overlapping tatami mats beneath a desk, a look reinforced by the Shoji-screen-like doors. Yet the rug's two colors add a whole new dimension to the cleanly styled space.

Complementing breezy wicker furniture with white cotton cushions, wall-to-wall natural sisal seems to bring the outdoors into a garden room. Because the natural sisal won't fade, it performs well in the room's unforgiving sunlight.

An oversized sisal rug warms the slate floor of a very organically designed great room. A smaller, colorful Oriental rug that matches the room's pillows is layered on top of the sisal between the sofas, further emphasizing the sitting area.

specialties

IF YOU'RE LOOKING for an inspired floor, consider the materials highlighted in this section—including concrete, leather, and steel— which are exemplary models of forward-thinking choices. They are relatively new to residential flooring, but you've probably seen these flooring materials in offices, shopping centers, and other commercial spaces. The materials take on a fresh look when used in the home.

Of all the specialties, concrete is the most prevalent material for new home floors. Although not inexpensive, concrete is relatively less costly than leather or steel and packs a powerful design punch. It also lends itself to experimentation. You can have seashells embedded in the concrete flooring of a beach house, for example, or small pebbles added in a home that looks out on a mountain stream. Leather can be quite luxurious and a bit indulgent when used as flooring. Envision a leather-floored den complete with a comfortable chair and your favorite books. A stainless floor, on the other hand, would be the perfect complement to a contemporary kitchen.

For a more budget-conscious approach, you might consider using a touch of one of these materials to accent your floor. For instance, if you like the look of metal, you could use a metallic border with a ceramic tiled floor. Or if you have your eye on leather tiles for a home library, you could create a leather-floored reading nook and use wood flooring for the rest of the room. Specialty flooring materials can now play a unique role in home flooring design.

Bands of amber-colored concrete cut across the eating area in front of a kitchen peninsula. A lighted toe-kick beneath the peninsula cabinetry illuminates the perimeter of the floor, highlighting its mottled texture.

Cast in place, wedges of neutrally colored concrete fluidly follow the unusually curved walls of a great room.

A *cast-concrete floor
in a sun-drenched
room mimics the look
of vintage terra-cotta
tiles—from pillowed
surfaces to wide
contrasting grout
lines—while providing
a more forgiving floor.*

*A floor of naturally
shaped leather lends
an air of timeworn
elegance to a living
room filled with
Mediterranean
antiques. Each piece
of leather is a slightly
different shade from
the adjacent one,
emphasizing each
individual shape.*

Square leather tiles bring a richness to the sitting area of an under-the-eaves bedroom. The floor's deep brown shading complements the room's creamy upholstered furniture. A wool area rug protects the floor from both direct sunlight and scuff marks.

Varied shades of natural leather floor tiles set the tone for an Asian-inspired living room filled with modern furniture. The leather floor abuts an interior rock garden. An area rug protects the room's main gathering place.

Triangular shapes of red leather form a uniquely creative floor for a loft dining room. Beyond the canvas that separates the dining space, hardwood floors run through the more highly trafficked areas of the loft.

A double row of
textured metallic
floor tiles follows
the perimeter of a
porcelain tile–covered
living room floor.
Metallic diamonds
inset between the
porcelain field tiles
repeat the theme across
the entire surface.

Steel foundry art tiles
bring renewed interest
to a traditional tiled
floor. The art tiles are
strategically placed in
the center of the floor,
where they provide the
most impact. As a
cost-saving measure,
no steel pieces are used
at the perimeter.

A SHOPPER'S GUIDE

CHOOSING FLOORING MATERIAL isn't necessarily easy. Not only is there a tremendous range of types of materials to choose from, but each type of flooring material also has its own subset of choices. The daunting task of choosing one (or maybe a mix of two or three types) might leave even a seasoned flooring expert a bit bewildered, especially if it was the expert's personal residence that was under renovation. But don't be overwhelmed by the fact that this is *your* home. Find the look that you like, and there is certain to be an appropriate solution for your floor. **THIS CHAPTER** is designed to help you make sense of all the options available for your floor. Now that you've browsed through the flooring images shown in the Great Ideas section, you probably have an idea of the flooring materials you like. Read on for more specific information on the flooring you're considering.

Ceramic Tile

A COOL-TO-THE-TOUCH CHAMELEON

There are two major types of ceramic floor tiles (also known as pavers): quarry tile, which is extruded from natural clay or shale, and tile made by the "pressed-dust" method, which includes ceramic and porcelain pavers.

Is it possible to tell which is which just by looking at a tile? Actually, yes. Since quarry tiles are made by an extrusion process, you can identify them by the grooves on their backs. Pressed tiles, on the other hand, have raised points or grids on the back.

Both types of ceramic tile are very strong, and both can be glazed or unglazed. In fact, glazed tiles can present a great number of design options. Some factories apply 15 or more layers of glaze material to a tile simply to make the tile look more natural.

Keep in mind that although you can use glazed tile on your floor, you need to check its glaze-wear rating. You don't want to place glazed tile in a high-traffic area where the glaze will wear down too quickly. On a scale from 0 to 5, a floor tile's glaze-wear rating can range from 2 for light traffic to a high-traffic 5.

Extruded to provide uniform density, rugged quarry tiles perform extremely well in high-traffic areas. Available in a range of earthy colors, sizes, and shapes, quarry tile can be glazed or unglazed, though unglazed is more popular.

Diagonally set sand-colored ceramic tiles designate the cooking area in a family kitchen. A pebbled mosaic border of stone separates the diagonal tiles from straight-on field tiles.

QUARRY TILE

Quarry tile

Most quarry tile comes unglazed in the clay colors of yellow, brown, rust, or red. It can be made very thick and therefore very strong. When it is extruded, a dense surface forms that reduces the staining and porosity of the unglazed surface. The resulting tile has a water absorption rate of less than 5 percent, which makes quarry tile a good candidate for high-traffic areas and hardworking kitchens. Unglazed quarry tile will last much longer than a glazed tile whose thin glazed surface will wear off eventually.

Ceramic pavers

Ceramic pavers made by the pressed-dust method can have a waterabsorption rate from 0 to 5 percent, but generally manufacturers make them with 2 to 3 percent absorption to improve bonding and to make cutting somewhat easier.

Glazed ceramic pavers can have textured, matte, painted, or photographic finishes. Unglazed pavers, such as earthy terra-cotta or saltillo tiles, will be more absorbent than their glazed cousins and should be sealed for protection against surface water and stains.

Porcelain pavers

One of the most misunderstood tiles, porcelain tiles have a water absorption rate of less than 0.5 percent. They are so dense they can be left unglazed and will last a very long time. Until recently, the color ranges and finishes of unglazed porcelain pavers were limited and considered more institutional, but that's no longer true.

CERAMIC TILE

PORCELAIN TILE

The popularity of stone has resulted in glazed ceramic pavers taking on its texture. A great variety of shapes and sizes is available in ceramic pavers, which usually have matching wall tiles.

Because of its durability, easy maintenance, and through-body color, porcelain is an ideal choice for a floor that replicates stone. Tiles can be finished with simple sanding, so chips are less likely to show.

PHOTOGRAPHY ON CERAMIC TILE

Porcelain pavers come in a wide range of styles and colors, emulating natural materials from terra-cotta to slate. The oversized formats of recently introduced porcelain pavers are also gaining favor.

So what's the catch? There are consequences to making a tile with a near-zero water absorption rate. Because of its density, porcelain tile needs to be physically supported while the adhesive sets. Also, porcelain tile is much harder to cut. You'll need a diamond wet-saw.

There is also a slight chance of staining with unglazed porcelains. Manufacturers are solving this by adding a clear glaze to the surface of the "unglazed" tile.

Mosaics

Mosaic tiles, once popular in prewar residences, are small porcelain tiles that measure about 2 ¼ by 2 ¼ inches at the maximum. They are generally sheet-mounted at the factory to save time in installation. They, too, are strong and have low water absorption.

Because they are small, mosaics can follow a contour, as in a shower floor. Mosaic tiles also allow for multiple drainage channels in wet areas to improve slip resistance. They recently have become quite popular as accents to larger tiles.

Glass

Often used as an accent to a ceramic tiled floor, glass is another material being constructed into tiles. Glass tiles are impervious to moisture, making them useful for kitchens and baths. And they can be eco-friendly too. Many companies are manufacturing glass tiles from recycled bottles and other glass products.

Trim units

Although not as ornamental as wall tile trims, paver trims are available to coordinate with tile flooring. Paver trims, such as bullnoses and cove bases, serve a functional purpose.

Many intricate mosaic designs and color combinations are available as pre-mounted sheets. It's rare today to see a hand-laid mosaic design. Some ceramic mosaics set in grout are available as large tiles.

They typically round out hard edges on stair treads. Or they can be used as a finish molding rising a few inches up the wall around the perimeter of the floor and along cabinet toe-kicks.

Color and shade variation

Because of the handcrafted nature of ceramic tiles, the Ceramic Tile Distributors Association (CTDA) has implemented a color/shade variation program. The CTDA found that some customers were disappointed when their tiles arrived in varying colors. Although these random variations are part of the beauty of a handcrafted tile, you might not want the diversity. Check the CTDA color/shade designation for your tile. It can range from V1 (uniform appearance) to V4 (substantial variation). If there is no CTDA designation, ask your dealer about the variations you can expect.

Also, when installing tile, it's good practice to blend the tiles from several boxes to avoid any shade shifts from lot to lot.

Slip resistance

There's no question—some ceramic tiles are slippery. Yet there are no national standards or requirements

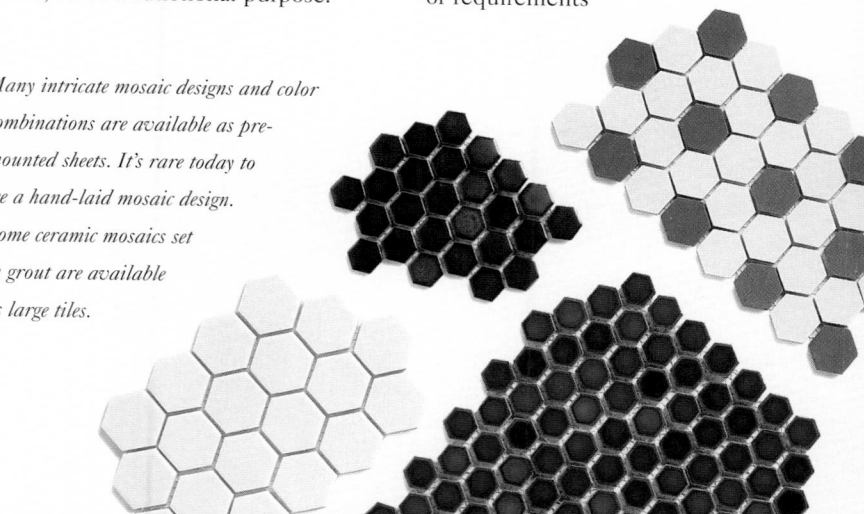

for slip resistance or coefficient of friction (COF). For practical purposes, however, the COF for floor tile is measured. Knowing the COF of your tile can help you make a sound choice at the beginning. For instance, the Americans with Disabilities Act (ADA) recommends a COF of 0.6 or greater on flat surfaces and 0.8 on ramps and inclines. If you have seniors or disabled persons in your household, you may want to take the COF into consideration.

There are also other ways to ensure a safe floor, such as choosing a tile that allows for well-placed grout lines or increasing the size of your grout joints.

A tiled floor can be made more slip resistant by applying slip-resistant coatings. The down side to having a no-slip floor? The more slip resistant a tile is, the harder it is to clean.

Care and cleaning

Because floor tile is water-resistant, spills and dirt stay on its surface. That makes tile pretty easy to clean. The best approach is first to sweep away or vacuum debris and scrape off any thick substances. You can use nylon scrubbing pads to remove stains from both tile and grout, but never use steel wool. Once the debris has been cleared, then damp-mop using a pH-neutral cleaner with no abrasives. One trick of the trade is to add glass cleaner or rubbing alcohol to your bucket of cleaning water to prevent streaks after it has dried.

To further protect your investment, you may need to seal certain types of tile, including some quarry tile, terra-cotta tile, and others. Grout sealers may be recommended for cement-based grouts. Ask your dealer if your floor requires sealing. Sealers need to be stripped and resealed periodically.

Installation

Because a ceramic tiled floor calls for a flat and rigid subfloor, it's likely that your contractor will begin by removing all your original flooring material. The contractor then will cover an uneven or damaged floor with an underlayment, typically cement backer board. Next, the contractor might assemble a few rows of tile to get an idea of how the overall pattern will fall. The next step is to comb out adhesive or pour a bed of mortar and set your tiles in it. The contractor will trim tiles as necessary. After all the tiles have been set, the contractor will grout the joints with a cement-based grout (or an epoxy grout when setting tile in areas

Reflecting the brilliance of gemstones, glass tiles can bring a translucent or iridescent quality to a room. They come in all sizes, shapes, and finishes, from glistening mosaics to opaque brick-shaped pavers. A few lines are crafted from recycled glass.

that will be subject to temperatures in excess of 100°F, such as shower stalls or on floors with radiant heating).

There should be a soft joint (or control joint) that is caulked, not grouted, when tile abuts another plane (or material), such as between a tub and the floor, in corners, or between wood and metal or tile. Control joints control where cracks may occur in your flooring system. Overall, it takes grout about a week to cure. Once the grout has cured, a grout sealer can be applied if needed.

Stone

NATURALLY REFINED AND SOPHISTICATED

For the most part, natural stone can be used anywhere that ceramic tile can be used. It can be left in its natural rough-hewn state or cut into geometric shapes, including mosaics. And thanks to new technologies, stone is now more competitively priced than ever before. Color and veining patterns are the major distinctions among natural stone. Limestone, marble, granite, slate, and terrazzo are the most common types of stone used for flooring. The one caveat is that the heavy weight of a masonry floor requires a well-supported subfloor.

RIGHT: Randomly set tumbled limestone tiles in two sizes cover the floor and tub facing of a master bath.

BELOW: Limestone tiles are available in a range of soft colors. Etched tiles and mosaic designs can be used as accents.

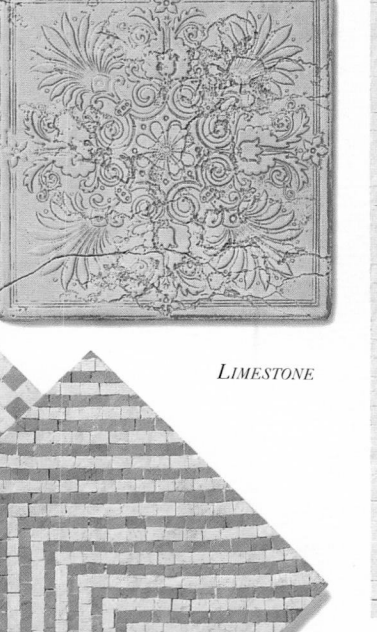

LIMESTONE

Limestone

Limestone does not show much grain-ing. It has a smooth, granular surface and varies in hardness. Although lime-stone is most often seen in creamy white or yellow tones, it also comes in black, gray, and brown. Limestone is more likely to stain than marble.

Marble

Marble, with its veining, is one of the most elegant stones, but susceptible to staining. Featuring one of the widest color ranges in natural stone, marble is available in black, cream, red, white, green, gold, gray, and pink. Some marbles are heavily veined, such as Nero Marquina with its ebony color and white veining, while others, such as Golden Spider, are lightly

TUMBLED MARBLE

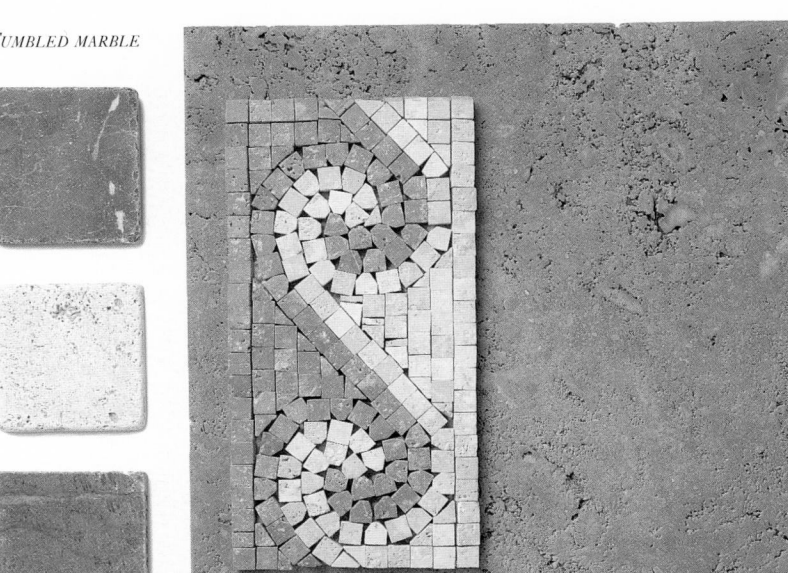

Perceived as one of the most formal flooring materials, marble has two distinct looks. As shown above, marble that has been either tumbled or antiqued has a soft texture. Polished marble in all its true color and veining, as shown below, looks luxurious.

POLISHED MARBLE

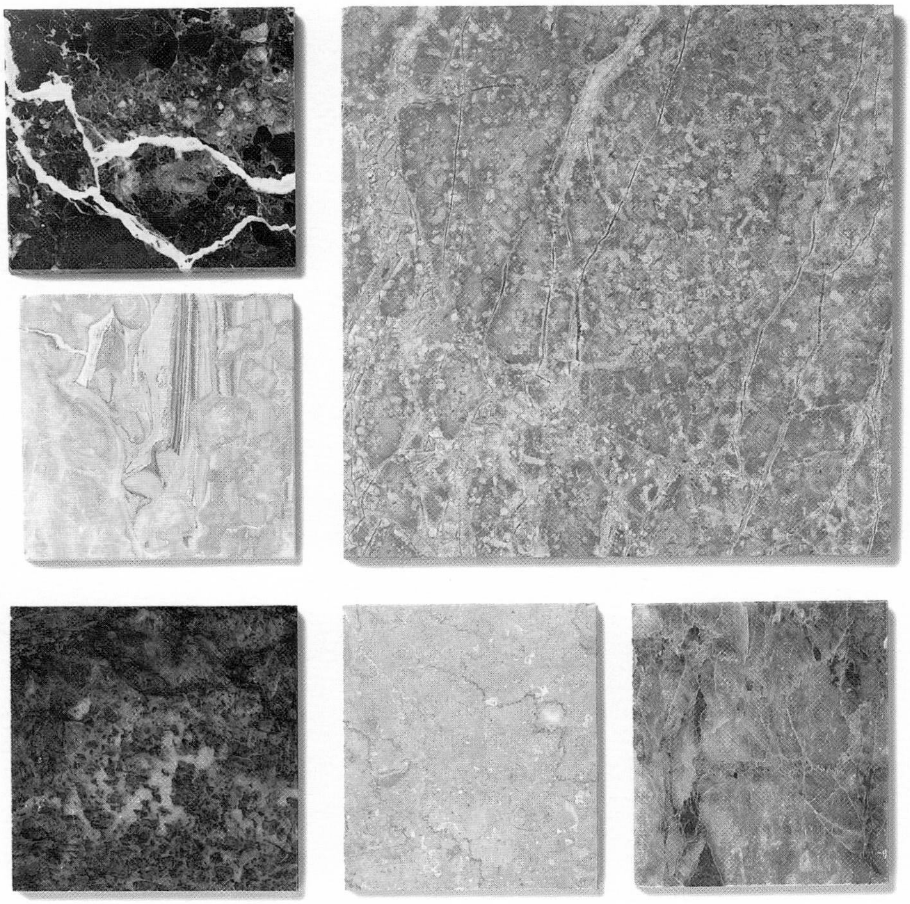

Often seen in shades of gray, slate tiles (above) are available in marvelous colors from reds to yellows to greens. Eye-catching patterns of granite (below) are favored in slab format, presenting a seamless floor.

SLATE

GRANITE

veined. Still others, such as Yellow Desert, look somewhat mottled, as if they were sponge finished. And there are also creamy soft classics, like Crema Marfil.

Slate

Slate, a fine-grained stone, tends to be thin and splits along natural grains and fissures, creating a rustic textured surface. Slate usually comes in black, gray, or green, but many interesting variations exist.

Granite

Granite is a close-grained rock with a mottled pattern often combining two or more colors and comes in hues from salt-and-pepper to rich rust tones to black. A very hard material, it is easier than marble to maintain. However, it is porous and will stain.

Terrazzo

Terrazzo, also known as agglomerate stone, is a man-made stone that features marble, granite, onyx, or glass chips anchored in a binder of cement or nonporous resin. Terrazzo can be poured in place or precast.

Flagstone

You might hear the term *flagstone* used in reference to stone paving. Flagstone is simply a generic term for flat slabs of paving stone, usually slate or limestone. These slabs often feature irregular edges and frequently are used outdoors for patios and pool decks, although many flooring

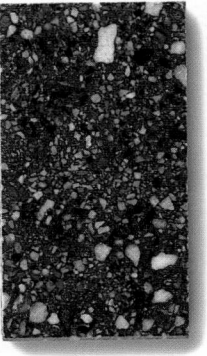
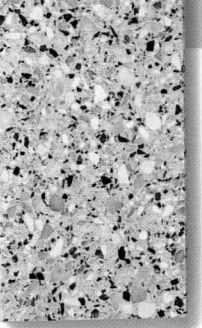

Terrazzo

The irregularly shaped chips in terrazzo, small or large, one color or multicolored, create a wealth of patterns and textures in this man-made stone.

designers are bringing this rustic look indoors to garden and sunrooms.

Surface finishes

Not only does a variety of natural stones exist, but there are six main types of surface finishes that you can choose from. More textured finishes are being favored today, as opposed to the high shine from past decades. Their gain can be attributed in part to better slip resistance, but it's due mainly to their matte appearance.

A honed finish has a flat to low sheen and appears very smooth, although it may be porous. A polished finish creates a glossy surface that brings out the color of a stone. A polished surface is very smooth and not very porous but will wear with time. A flamed finish creates a rough surface developed through intense heat. The surface is very porous. A tumbled finish, created by tumbling pieces of stone, results in a slightly rough, worn texture. A sandblasted finish results from blasting stone with a pressurized flow of water and sand.

It creates a textured surface with a matte gloss. A sawn finish shows the rough, circular path of a diamond-tipped saw blade. A bash-hammered finish is a textured surface created by a pounding action.

Water-jet options

You might see precut stone medallions, borders, or inlays when shopping for flooring. These look fabulous and will add a custom touch to your floor. New water-jet cutting techniques allow these special pieces to be crafted quickly and affordably. Usually designs are created first on computer. Then the design is used to guide the water jets through the stone cutting.

Care and cleaning

Dust-mop your stone floor frequently with a clean, untreated, dry dust mop, and it will last for many years. Dirt and grit do the most damage to a stone floor. Area rugs inside and outside an entrance will help keep abrasives to a minimum. Blot up spills immediately, and use a pH-neutral detergent or

stone soap to clean your floor. Do not use vinegar or lemon juice.

Sealants

To protect against staining and acid damage, you should apply a sealant on porous stones and finishes. You can choose to seal minimally with a stone soap or more intently with a penetrating sealer and a hard wax. Whatever sealer you select, test its appearance on a sample of your stone before applying it to the floor.

Installation

The irregularity of natural stone calls for a thick cushion of mortar to compensate for varying thickness. If working with a wood subfloor, your contractor may want to protect it with felt and possibly a layer of wire mesh to prevent the mortar from cracking. Your contractor will likely work in sections, spreading the mortar in stages. The mortar should set for 24 hours. Then the joints will be filled with similar mortar. A sealer can be applied once the mortared joints have dried.

Wood

AN AGE-OLD CLASSIC WITHSTANDS THE TEST OF TIME

When you choose wood, you're choosing one of the warmest, most time-tested, and versatile flooring materials. And one that looks better with time.

Types of wood

Many wood species are used for flooring. Each one has its own natural color, markings, and advantages.

OAK flooring comes in either white or red. The color of white oak runs from a creamy white or light brown to medium brown. It's a bit harder than red oak, has smaller markings, and has a more uniform appearance. Red oak is reddish brown, and its open grain makes it somewhat porous.

MAPLE flooring runs from pale white to light reddish brown. It has a uniform texture and closed grain and is very hard, harder than red oak.

PINE, considered a softwood rather than a hardwood like oak or maple, was commonly used in early American flooring because of its natural stability. Longleaf heart pine (on a par with red oak) and southern yellow pine are the hardest of all pines. Minor dents and dings will happen over time but tend to enhance a floor's character.

BAMBOO flooring is similar to oak in dent resistance and is much more dimensionally stable than most wood flooring. Because bamboo is harvested from grass and rejuvenates itself to maturity in three to five years, it is envi-

Strips of reddish-brown Bankirai, a smooth and very durable tropical wood from Indonesia, on the floor of a living room will ultimately weather to an even richer shade.

ronmentally friendly. It comes in both vertical and flat-grain patterns and in a light natural and a darker amber color.

CHERRY is appreciated for its warm reddish coloring, straight grain, and smooth texture. It looks sleek when sanded and finished and is frequently used for cabinetry. Of medium density, it is dimensionally stable upon kiln drying.

MAHOGANY, an extremely durable high-density wood, has a deep reddish brown color and very fine graining. Mahogany encompasses a

few different timber species. It was first discovered in the West Indies but now, due to sustainable harvesting, comes from Mexico, and Central and South America.

TEAK, similar in strength to oak, is naturally resistant to insects, fungus, termites, and temperature shifts. Recently brought back into vogue through sustainable sources, it has a distinct shading that varies from yellowish brown to dark golden brown. Its grain runs straight, although its texture can be uneven.

Types of construction

Wood floors can be made from solid wood, from engineered wood, or from reclaimed wood.

Solid wood is any wood that is one piece from top to bottom. It performs best in a moisture-controlled environment. Engineered wood flooring is made of cross-stacked layers of base wood with a veneer top layer of your choice of wood. Engineered wood flooring is more dimensionally stable and can be installed where solid wood cannot because of moisture. Reclaimed or recycled woods are made from boards salvaged from old buildings or river bottoms. The salvaged pieces can be 60 to 70 years old and sometimes come with a history. Since this wood usually comes from old-growth forests, it is harder and denser than new-growth wood. Typical reclaimed species include chestnut, hickory, cherry, and oak.

Sizes

Wood flooring started as planks or wide boards; then the standard moved to 2¼-inch-wide strips and later to 1½-inch strips. Now there's a broad range available. Strip flooring still ranges from 1½ to 2¼ inches wide. Plank flooring ranges from 3 to 8 inches wide. Parquet is another form of wood flooring that involves decorative cuts of wood pieced together to

---

Many popular wood species are being used for floors today. Each one shown here is its natural color—no stains were used—and has its own particular markings. Wood can be chosen by color or level of hardness.

RUSTIC HICKORY PECAN

FUMED WHITE OAK

OAK

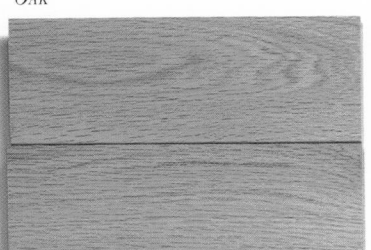

MAHOGANY

VERTICAL BAMBOO

BRAZILIAN CHERRY

MAPLE

TEAK

HORIZONTAL BAMBOO

AMERICAN CHERRY

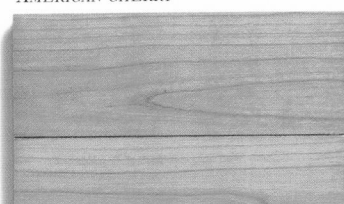

GEOMETRIC FIELD PATTERNS AND CORNER DESIGNS

create a geometric design. The pieces are usually held in place by nails or with adhesives or with both.

Grade

Different species of woods have different standards. The higher the grade, the clearer the wood. Oak has three basic grades. Select oak is mostly clear, but shows some natural characteristics, such as knots and color variations. No. 1 Common oak shows light and dark colors, knots, flags, and wormholes. No. 2 Common oak is even more rustic. Maple has three grades ranging from Clear, with limited character marks, to No. 1 Common and No. 2 Common, with more characteristics of the species. There are various grades as well as hardnesses of pine flooring. Within each type of pine—yellow, white, or heart, the grades range from a rustic country look with all of the wood's characteristics to a clear wood.

Cut

The angle that a saw cuts a piece of wood determines its cut. The three standard hardwood cuts include plainsawn, quartersawn, and riftsawn. Plainsawn, which shows growth ring patterns, is the most common.

Quartersawn wood is more refined and less susceptible to moisture, but it's also more costly. Riftsawn wood is cut at an angle slightly different from quartersawn wood.

Finishes and treatments

To finish a wood floor, you can choose a surface finish made of synthetic resin or use a penetrating stain or wax. Surface finishes are available in high-gloss, semigloss, satin, and matte. But your choices don't end there. Surface finishes include oil-modified urethane, moisture-cured urethane, conversion varnish, and water-based urethane. Moisture-cured urethane is the most durable of these finishes, yet it's the hardest to apply. With a two- to three-hour drying time, water-based urethane dries the fastest.

Penetrating stains and waxes will soak into the pores of your wood floor and harden to form a protective seal. If you wax your floor, you should only use cleaning products specifically made for wax finishes. Also recognize that these same stains can be used to mimic the inlays of exotic woods.

As wood floors grow more popular, many homeowners are turning to faux finishes for cost-effective custom looks. You can paint hardwood floors of any type, whether they are old or new and whether the finish was applied on-site or in the factory. Paint professionals recommend water-based paints for best results.

Although experts caution you may weaken your floor, wood flooring can be bleached for effect too. Bleaching wood involves brushing the wood with caustic soda or ammonia and applying hydrogen peroxide.

If you're looking for a whitish finish, pickling may be a better choice. By rubbing white paint into your wood flooring, pickling will highlight its markings.

Inlays

Ready-to-install, prefabricated wood tiles with medallions, starbursts, and borders are available through most wood flooring dealers. Most of these off-the-shelf designs are laser-cut creations. At one time, such designs needed to be hand-cut and so were quite costly. These prefabricated pieces let you affordably mix and match to create your own patterns. Preplanning your floor design is crucial if you decide to use an inlay.

Care and cleaning

Dirt, grit, and sand pose the main threat to a hardwood floor. They act like sandpaper on a floor's finish, resulting in scratches, dents, and dulling. Placing floor mats or area rugs at your home's entrances will help trap dirt and prevent damage. It's also important that you wipe up spills right away, and when you vacuum be sure to use a vacuum with a brush attachment, not a beater bar. After vacuuming or sweeping, you may damp-mop your floor using a neutral-pH wood cleaner. If your floor is sealed properly, water won't damage it.

Installation

To allow your wood flooring to acclimate, it will probably be delivered to you about four days before installation. The most popular way to install a solid wood floor is to nail down unfinished solid wood flooring to a wood subfloor (usually $3/4$-inch plywood) or joists (or glue parquet tiles directly to a concrete slab), then sand it and apply a finish. If you can bear the dust and fumes, this method provides the most design options. Wood flooring can be made to lie end to end, or it can have a tongue-and-groove construction that fits together like a puzzle. Prefinished flooring is sanded and finished in the factory, cutting on-site job time by at least half. Floating installations, in which planks are joined to one another rather than a subfloor, are used for engineered wood floors. Some engineered wood flooring can be nailed down, which requires a wood subfloor.

LASER-CUT BORDER DESIGNS

Resilient

EASY CARE AND GOOD LOOKS, TOO!

New advances have made resilient flooring more appealing than ever. Not only have protective finishes been developed that make resilient flooring more durable, but manufacturers are employing new technologies to replicate traditional flooring materials, including stone, slate, and tile. At the same time they are enhancing the unique properties of resilient flooring. Embossing and luminescence give dimension to resilient flooring, while metallic finishes are being used as accents. The most popular resilient flooring is vinyl, but linoleum has recently made a comeback in its full retro glory. Cork and rubber also fall under the resilient flooring category. More custom design options are available if you choose a commercial resilient. For a custom design, you'll need the help of a designer.

Vinyl

Vinyl flooring comes in tiles or sheets, features a foam or vinyl core layered on a backing, and is finished with a design layer protected by a wear surface. Or vinyl flooring can be inlaid with vinyl granules fused on a backing of vinyl or felt. A vinyl backing will offer more resilience.

There are three types of vinyl surfaces: no-wax, urethane, and enhanced urethane. No-wax resists scuffs, scrapes, and some stains but requires occasional polishing.

Urethane surfaces will stand up better to scuffs, scrapes, and stains. They hold their polished finish longer than a no-wax finish.

Enhanced urethane outperforms both no-wax and urethane surfaces.

Linoleum

Linoleum was invented in the late nineteenth century and extensively used as flooring in tiles and sheets until the 1960s. This durable material, being made from flax, is ecologically sound. The name *linoleum* comes from *linum* (Latin for flax) and *oleum* (which means oil). Linseed oil, which is derived from flax and rosin, is oxidized to create linoleum cement. This cement is then mixed with wood flour and limestone and poured over sheets of jute backing material. It is allowed to cure to reach the desired flexibility and resilience.

Cork

Cork, which comes from the outer bark of oak trees, has been used as a flooring material for more than a century.

Cork flooring is durable, provides acoustical and thermal insulation, and is resistant to moisture and decay. It is harvested from trees in a sustainable manner and comes either as cork floor tiles or most recently as tongue-and-groove cork flooring.

VINYL.

Rubber

The inherent properties of rubber flooring tiles are durability, natural resiliency, and low maintenance. Like cork, rubber is dimensionally stable, sound absorbent, and recyclable. As its styling improves and the number of design profiles grows, rubber flooring is gaining favor in homes. It's great for wet areas and recreation rooms. Some rubber flooring claims to self-heal from scratches and abrasions.

Care and cleaning

The trick to keeping resilient flooring in good shape is good preventive care. You need to protect your floor against indentations and furniture damage. Make sure your furniture legs have large-surface, nonstaining floor protectors. Glides should be covered with felt pads. Also check to see that rubber wheels are nonstaining.

You will need to protect a resilient floor from dirt. Using mats at your home's entrances will help keep grit to a minimum. You'll need to be sure that your mats feature latex backing rather than rubber, which may stain your floor. Because extreme heat and sun pose a threat to a resilient floor, you need to draw your window coverings during strong

LINOLEUM

sunlight to minimize fading. On a regular basis, you'll need only to sweep or vacuum your floor and then mop it with a pH-neutral cleaner.

Installation

Resilient flooring needs 24 hours to acclimate before it's cut. Afterward, an installer will either trim resilient sheet flooring in place or cut from a template of the room, allowing for expansion due to changes in humidity. There's usually no need to remove existing flooring if it's in good condition. In fact, if your existing floor is an old resilient floor, it might be advisable not to remove it because some old resilient products contain asbestos (today's resilient flooring does not contain asbestos).

Most resilient tile is self-adhesive, basically peel and stick. If your new sheet flooring requires a seam and is being applied over an old floor, the installer will offset the two seams. The installer will then either apply adhesive to the entire surface area or to the perimeter of the floor, and use a roller to tightly bond the flooring to the subfloor, and a seam sealer to bond the seams.

RUBBER

CORK

Laminate

EUROPEAN STYLING MEETS EASY MAINTENANCE

Laminate flooring was originally developed in Sweden during the early 1980s, making it one of the newest flooring materials available. Constructed of a sturdy core made of recycled materials, laminated with several layers of paper, topped by a design layer, and finished with a protective coating, it is valued for its durability, ease of installation, and ease of maintenance. Some early concerns arose regarding laminate flooring that chipped or delaminated and about the hollow sound produced when laminates were walked on. In response to those complaints, laminate flooring has improved significantly over the last 20 years. Today's laminate amazingly resists dents, burns, and stains. Pads have been developed to place beneath laminate flooring to absorb the sound of footsteps. Best of all, laminate

A laminate floor looks like smooth hardwood planking. Laminate panels are laid perpendicular to one another to designate a transition into an adjacent room. Base trim conceals the expansion areas.

STONE LAMINATE

WOOD LAMINATE

flooring now can be used in any room, including kitchens and baths.

With these and other improvements, warranties have been extended from 10 years to 15, then to triple 15 (warranty against stains, wear, and water damage), then to 25 years, and now to lifetime. Some manufacturers have divided their lines into different grades to reflect warranty length.

Styling

Laminate styling also has improved greatly. At first, all laminated floors emulated wood flooring, simply because that was the material in demand at the time. Since it's the top design layer that features the image of your desired flooring, almost any type of material can be replicated. Now you can choose many variations of

wood looks, from birch to maple to walnut, including patterns such as herringbone and checks, and blocked and plank floors. Imitation stone laminates mimic varying shades of marble, granite, limestone, and more.

Trim pieces

Laminate floor systems include all the accoutrements you'll need to finish your floor. Laminate wall bases and quarter rounds come in colors and finishes that complement the floor. There are also transition moldings for use where a laminate floor meets a different flooring material, such as carpet, tile, stone, or wood. Laminate threshold moldings are available to use in doorways, as are step moldings for staircases.

Care and cleaning

To protect a laminate floor, it's important that you place area rugs or mats at

the entrances to your home and use felt protectors and rubber casters on furniture. Other than that, a laminate floor will require only sweeping or vacuuming and damp-mopping. For tough stains, such as ink, it's safe to use nail polish remover or alcohol on laminate. There is no need for stripping or waxing a laminate floor.

Installation

Laminate flooring can be installed over almost any existing flooring, so long as it is smooth and well bonded. Unlike traditional wood floors, laminate floors are installed as "floating floors." Simply put, the floor is not physically attached to the subfloor. Adhesive attaches the laminate boards to one another only. There are also tongue-and-groove laminates that don't require adhesives. They just click into place. Expansion areas are left along the perimeter of the finished floor, allowing it to expand and contract as necessary with temperature and humidity changes. The expansion areas are concealed by the wall base trim.

Carpet

NOT YOUR TYPICAL WALL-TO-WALL ANYMORE

Carpeting is available in a greater variety of patterns, color combinations, and constructions than ever before. In addition to providing design, carpeting enhances your home by absorbing sound, insulating against cold, cushioning your feet, and helping to prevent slips and falls. Carpets come either as broadloom for wall-to-wall applications or prebound as area rugs.

When shopping for carpet, look for performance rating guidelines. These ratings are based on traffic performance. Typically, they are based on a 5-point scale, with 4 or 5 being best for the highest-traffic areas.

Fiber

Fiber is carpet's basic ingredient. There are five basic types of carpet pile fibers: nylon, olefin, polyester, acrylic, and wool. Plant fibers such as sisal offer another choice. Fibers can be blended to combine the best characteristics of each in one carpet. For instance, sisal can be blended with wool for optimal feel and wear resistance. Most carpeting in the United States is made of nylon, and for good reason: It is wear resistant and resilient, withstands the weight and movement of furniture, and comes in many colors. It also resists soils and stains.

Leather trims the border of a natural-color wool area rug featuring dual-level loop construction, a design that replicates the look of sisal carpeting.

Sisal

Natural-fiber sisal is a great neutral floor covering but should be used only in dry areas because it is susceptible to moisture and staining. It can get slippery and is not recommended for stairs.

Olefin (or polypropylene) is also a strong fiber. It, too, resists wear and stains and static electricity. It holds up well against moisture, which makes it suitable for indoor/outdoor rooms.

Polyester maintains its color and looks the most lush when used in thick, cut-pile textures. Polyester is also easy to clean and resistant to water-soluble stains.

Acrylic looks like wool and costs much less. It has a low static level and is moisture and mildew resistant.

Wool has been touted through the ages for its overall performance. It is soft, has high bulk, and comes in many colors. However, it can be more expensive than synthetic fibers.

Pile

The construction of a carpet's pile gives it a distinct texture and pattern. There are three main construction techniques: level loop, multilevel loop, and cut pile. Sometimes, in much the same way fibers are blended in a carpet, these techniques are combined to add even more dimension.

Level-loop pile features loops at the same height. It is informal and includes the popular Berber carpets. It doesn't show footprints, so it works in high-traffic areas. In general, the tighter the loop, the more durable the carpet.

Multilevel-loop pile, with loop heights at two or three different levels, creates interesting patterns. It, too, is durable and has a casual look.

Cut-pile carpet means that the loops are cut, creating tufts of yarn. It has a more formal look. The type of fiber, density of tufts, and amount of twist in the yarn all play a role in the durability of a cut-pile carpet.

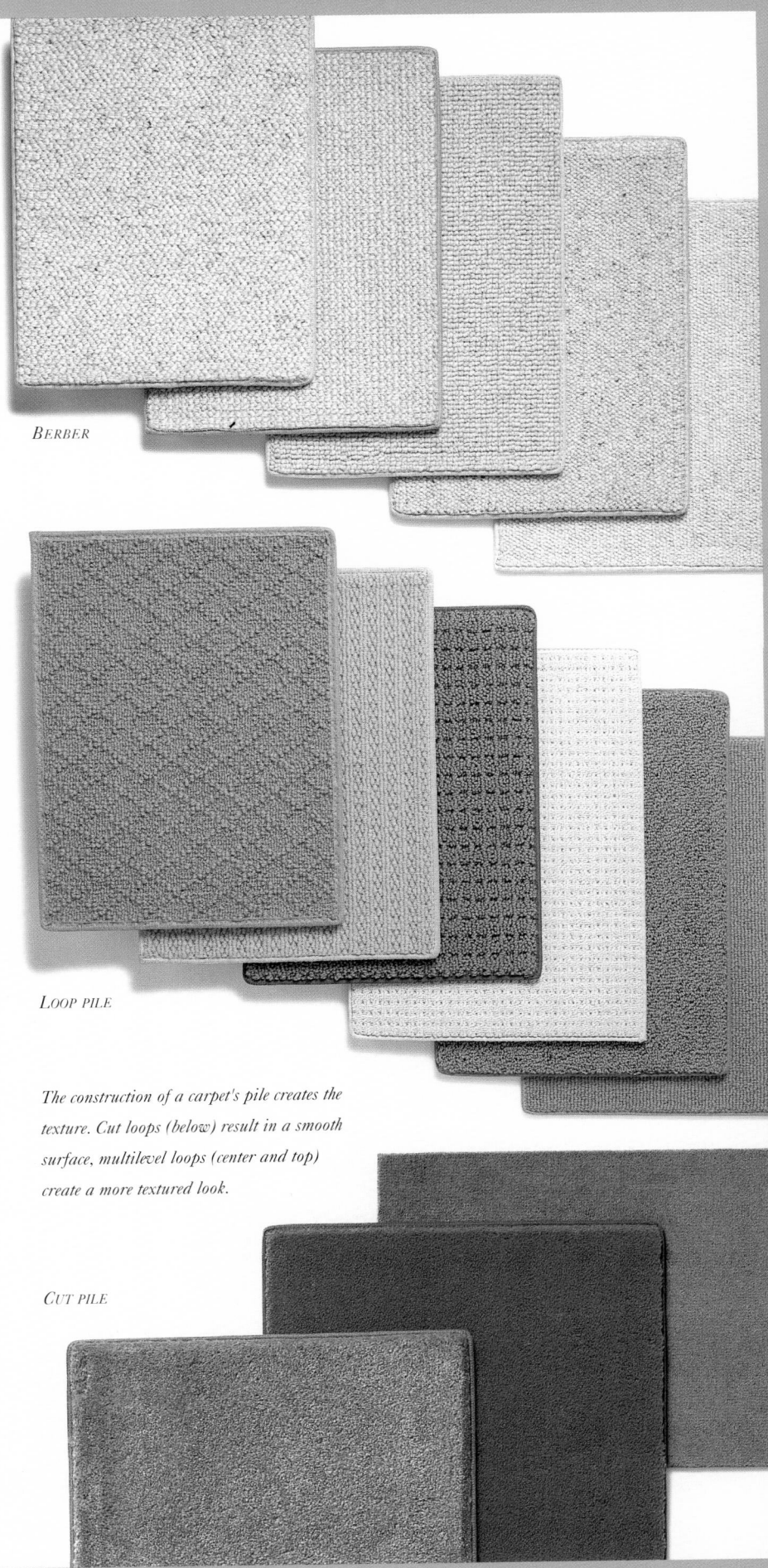

BERBER

LOOP PILE

The construction of a carpet's pile creates the texture. Cut loops (below) result in a smooth surface, multilevel loops (center and top) create a more textured look.

CUT PILE

Care and cleaning

Many carpets today come with stain protection, soil protection, and static resistance. New stain- and soil-resistant technology makes carpeting and rugs much easier to clean, but it's still important to remove stains as quickly as possible. Always absorb wet spills by blotting, not rubbing. Most home-owners steam-clean their carpets once a year. In between, regular vacuuming is recommended.

Custom options

To further broaden your options, some carpeting manufacturers are offering custom work for both area rugs and broadloom (wall-to-wall). That means you can virtually create your own design using such elements as borders or have your carpet dyed to match whatever color you like. You can also ask for custom binding to finish the edges of your carpet. Carpeting can be bound to any size you need, whether you're looking for an area rug or a wall-to-wall carpet that can be easily removed as necessary. You can also choose a binding material to match or contrast with the carpet, depending on your preference.

Carpet cushion

Using carpet cushion under a carpet makes it feel and look better longer and helps improve insulation. Carpet cushion is made from polyurethane foam, fiber, or rubber, or from recycled materials. The type and thickness of the cushion you'll need varies according to traffic patterns. Bedrooms, dens, lounge areas, and other rooms with light or moderate traffic can use thicker and softer cushion, while living rooms, hallways, stairs, and other heavy-traffic areas require thinner cushion. A quality sisal, however, will be backed with thick latex and won't require cushioning.

Installation

Carpeting can be installed over wood or concrete. First, the installer fastens tackless strips around the room's perimeter. If carpet cushion is desired, it is put down and stretched to fit. Then the carpet is cut to a manageable size. After rolling out the carpet for the majority of the room, the installer cuts additional pieces for

ABOVE: Available in both neutrals and colorful shades, a basic blend of loop and cut-pile construction can be used to execute unique patterns on broadloom carpeting.

RIGHT: Geometric patterns in broadloom carpet in a range of colors create a subtle design on which the décor of the room can rest.

curves and niches. Seams are created where pieces of carpet meet. Using a knee kicker, the installer attaches the carpet to one wall of tackless strips. Using a power stretcher, the carpet is stretched to fit the room. Finally, the installer trims the carpet more closely and cuts out obstacles. In some cases, such as sisal, a direct glue-down installation is recommended in place of tackless strips.

RIGHT: *The shag carpet is back. Shading is more subtle than before, but now there are choices in the lengths of shaggy cut pile, ranging from short and conservative, called frieze, to long and adventurous, called rya.*

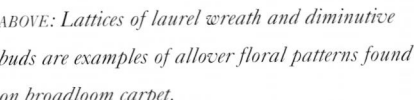

ABOVE: *Lattices of laurel wreath and diminutive buds are examples of allover floral patterns found on broadloom carpet.*

RIGHT: *A closed-loop area rug combining a floral border with a geometric field could be the focal point in a room. Keep in mind that as long as colors coordinate, carpeting patterns need not match other fabrics in the room.*

Specialties

FOR THE FASHION-FORWARD SET

I f you're feeling adventurous when it comes to your floor, specialty flooring offers interesting options. While these specialties may seem new to you, they've been used commercially for years. Think of your favorite boutique store or funky downtown restaurant. You're sure to see great examples of specialty flooring there. They come with some outstanding properties. So if your budget permits experimentation, don't hesitate to check out these alternatives.

Concrete

Concrete's not just for your ordinary gray driveway anymore. Because of its flexibility, it can take on color, texture, and shape, mimicking other, more costly flooring materials. And it offers long-term performance.

Concrete flooring comes precast, cast-in-place, or in the form of concrete floor tiles. It can be poured right over a concrete slab structure. Portland cement, water, sand, and coarse aggregate are proportioned and mixed to produce concrete flooring. Because its hardening process continues for years, concrete gets stronger as it gets older.

Concrete may be colored by adding pigments before or after it is in place, by using chemical stains, or by exposing aggregates, such as marble, granite chips, or pebbles, at the surface. Textured finishes can vary from rough

Poured-in-place concrete covers the floor of a creatively designed kitchen. Natural concrete is inset with wedges of colored concrete in shades of amber, taupe, and green. The colors pick up the brushed steel from the kitchen island and the warm honeyed hues of the maple cabinetry.

to polished. Patterns can be scored, stamped, rolled, or inlaid into the concrete. Some designers have been known to use divider strips (most commonly redwood) to form panels of various sizes and shapes.

The best way to maintain a concrete floor is to have it sealed. Urethane, epoxy, or water-based sealers are your typical choices. Once the sealer is applied, cleaning is as simple as sweeping and damp-mopping.

LEATHER

Leather

Leather floor tile is made from the same material as leather-soled shoes. Just like its apparel counterpart, the leather for flooring is tanned and dyed with aniline dye. Well-made leather flooring features a waxed finish that is heated into the material. Available in numerous colors and sizes, leather flooring will develop a patina over time. It possesses great sound-insulating properties and is warm to the touch. It can be used throughout the home but is not recommended for high-moisture areas, including kitchens and baths, or high-traffic areas, such as entrances. You'll probably also want to install a leather floor in areas out of direct sunlight.

It's easier than you'd expect to keep a leather floor clean. You'll need to vacuum your leather floor with a soft brush attachment weekly. Once a month, you can damp-mop your floor. Annual waxing is recommended.

Metal

Metal flooring runs the gamut from sleek stainless steel tiles to industrial-type grated floors. Steel is frequently used for open staircases because of its structural superiority. In addition, metallic composite materials have evolved into tiles that look just like steel, bronze, and other metals. They are primarily used as accents to other flooring materials, such as wood, ceramic, or stone. Because metals typically contain recycled products, they are considered environmentally friendly.

Cleaning a metal floor calls for sweeping with a soft-bristled broom or dust-mopping to remove any loose particles, then damp-mopping with a nonabrasive pH-neutral cleaner.

METAL

Metal veneer on composite tiles, top right, as well as solid cast-metal tiles and cast-metal medallions set in concrete, serve as unique flooring accents.

photo
credits

Abet Laminati: 84 top
Aged Woods, Inc.: 65
American Olean: 26; 41
Ann Sacks: 12 top right; 30; 36 bottom; 42; 50–51; 55 bottom; 101 bottom
Armstrong World Industries, Inc.: 81; 82–83
Artistic Tile, Inc. (1-800-260-8646; www.artistictile.com): 10 bottom; 56 bottom
Bisazza Glass Tile: 36 top
Blackstock Leather, Inc. (1-800-663-6657; www.blackstockleather.com): 99 (Photograph by Doug Hall); 100 top (Photograph by David Lee) and bottom (Photograph by Paul Warchol)
Bomanite Corporation: 13 bottom right; 96; 97; 98 top; 124

Bruce hardwood floors: title page; 12 bottom; 17; 27; 59; 60 bottom; 64 top; 66; 68; 112; 126
Congoleum Corporation: 10 top; 14; 74 top; 75; 77 top
Crossville Porcelain Stone/USA: 32
Engelmann, Inc. Contractors, Sun Valley, Idaho: 62 top; 108
Phillip Ennis: 38 bottom (Nicholas Calder); 45 (Terra Designs/Anna Salibelo); 46–47 (IDT/Stuart Narofsky); 48 top (Angela Grande Associates with Claus, Architect) ; 49 (Nicholas Calder); 52 bottom (Dineen Nealy Architects); 57; 93 (Denise Balaser); 104 (John Buscarello)
Forbo Linoleum, Inc.: 73; 74 bottom
Formica Corporation: 16; 60; 80; 83; 84 bottom; 86; 87

Tria Giovan: 56 top
Ken Gutmaker: 85
Jamie Hadley: 123 bottom right
Imagine Tile, Inc.: 40 top and bottom
Dennis Krukowski: 33 (Siskin Valls, Inc.); 60 top (George Constant, Inc.)
Masland Carpets & Rugs: 11; 20; 21; 91
E. Andrew McKinney: 13 bottom left; 44; 64 bottom; 72; 90 bottom; 92 top and bottom; 95 top and bottom; 98 bottom; 120 top; 118 top
Melabee M Miller: 6 (Fentell Housing Corp., Vorhees, NJ); 13 top right and (Deborah Leamann Interiors, Pennington, NJ); 53 (Sharon Draznin, Short Hills, NJ); 67 top (Lisa Melone, Summit, NJ);

90 top (Deborah Leamann Interiors, Pennington, NJ)
Nafco, by Domco Tarkett: 76; 77 bottom
National Wood Flooring Association: 58; 61
Bradley Olman: 69 top and bottom
Questech® Metals from Crossville Porcelain Stone/USA: 101 top
Kenneth Rice Photography/ www.kenricephoto.com: 70 bottom
Mark Samu: 34 (Len Kurkowski A.I.A.); 35 bottom (Eileen Boyd Design); 39 (The Tile Studio); 43 top (Courtesy Hearst Publications); 52 top (Anne Tarasoff Design); 67 bottom (Courtesy Hearst Publications); 70 top (Courtesy Hearst Publications); 89 (Lee Najman)
Seneca Tiles, Inc. (1-800-426-4335; www.SenecaTiles.com): 102 (T.A. Etter Photography)
Alan Shortall 2001: copyright page; 8; 9; 12 top left; 19; 22; 35 top; 48 bottom; 54; 55 top and bottom; 94
Tim Street-Porter/beateworks.com: 38 top (Scott Johnson Architect); 71 (Brian Murphy Architect)
Tarkett, Inc.: 4; 13 top left
Through the Lens Management/ R. Greg Hursley: 28
TimberGrass Fine Bamboo Flooring & Panels, Bainbridge Island, WA: 62 bottom; 63 (Photographs by Art Grice)
Jessie Walker Associates: 5 (David Smith, Designer); 18 (Michael Muha of M.G. Michael & Associates, Inc., Birmingham, MI); 31 and back cover; 37 (Steve Knutson of Knutson Designs, Evanston, IL); 43 bottom (Past Basket, Dave McFadden, Designer, Geneva, IL); 47 (Allen Portnoy, ASID, Chicago, IL); 88 (Kay McCarthy, Designer; Jim Thorp, Architect, Burr Ridge, IL)
Wicanders Cork Flooring: 15; 25; 78–79; 79 top and bottom

index